Microsoft Dynamics AX Interview Questions

Compiled by ITCOOKBOOK

Microsoft Dynamics AX

ISBN: 978-1-60332-004-7

Edited By: Jamie Fisher

Printed in the United States of America

Please visit our website at www.itcookbook.com

Table of Contents

Introduction..8

Axapta General Discussion..10

   Question 1: Visual SourceSafe and MDAX 4.0....................11
   Question 2: Sub-contract in AX4...12
   Question 3: ABC Codes...13
   Question 4: User Admin is not connected to employee.........14
   Question 5: Axapta Object Server 4.0 not restarting.............15
   Question 6: Reporting Server Role for AX 4.0......................18
   Question 7: Enterprise Portal Error message.........................19
   Question 8: Can't find Rapid Configuration Toolkit (RCT)
   anymore...21
   Question 9:
   Microsoft.Dynamics.BusinessConnectorNet.Axapta in
   BatchRuns..22
   Question 10: Active Directory import wizard.........................23
   Question 11: AX4 SP 1 Location wizard.................................23
   Question 12: Delete BOM records..24
   Question 13: Changing the language in Axapta 4.0...............24
   Question 14: 4.0 SP1 User session no longer valid 25
   Question 15: Invite multiple attendees in MDY AX CRM-
   module...26
   Question 16: Synchronizing Data-Dictionary-ERROR..........27
   Question 17: Maintenance Strategy.......................................28
   Question 18: Rename AOS instance..30
   Question 19: Deploying webparts on a Sharepoint site 30
   Question 20: Warning: Application Event Viewer.................31
   Question 21: Unable to create an Enterprise Portal 32
   Question 22: Importing BOMs from Excel............................34
   Question 23: Sync error in AX4.0...35
   Question 24: KR2/KR3 Installation.......................................35
   Question 25: AIF...36
   Question 26: Removing an Enterprise Portal Site
   Documentation..38
   Question 27: Remove accents from strings...........................39
   Question 28: Best Practice Checks meaning..........................40
   Question 29: VendPaymProposal, find a specific spectrans. .41
   Question 30: Close All Open Forms..42
   Question 31: Take out AX4.0 Find filter (Ctrl-K) pre-
   populated text...42
   Question 32: Active Directory Import....................................43

Question 33: Duplicate qualifications not allowed in Axapta HR..44
Question 34: AX4.0: Database transfer...........................45
Question 35: Authentication problems 46
Question 36: Axapta 3 to AX 4 upgrade documentation.......48
Question 37: Overlap time.......................................49
Question 38: Production costing, Inventory closing..............50
Question 39: Production costing.................................51
Question 40: Text file to be generated via Axapta.................52
Question 41: SQL 2005 Enterprise Client Required for Axapta v3 AOS environment...53
Question 42: Forecast Consumption in Axapta....................54
Question 43: AX 4.0: no more aoc-files?...........................55
Question 44: Dedicated link from AOS to SQL DB...............56
Question 45: Kernel Rollup - Best Practice.......................57
Question 46: Multi-channel order processing......................58
Question 47: AOS licenses.......................................58
Question 48: ActiveX Error in Application Object Tree 59
Question 49: Migration to V4 from V3 SP4...........................60
Question 50: AX Team Server Setup Installation Error........61

Axapta Applications...62

Question 51: Delete Ended Production orders......................63
Question 52: Axapta Batch Server Installation 63
Question 53: AX and NAV.......................................64
Question 54: Automatic Processing of Sales Orders.............65
Question 55: Ax 4.0: Usage of OLD folder...........................66
Question 56: Set up of Transfer Orders in 4.01 67
Question 57: Project and type Fixed-Price...........................68
Question 58: Error creating production journal..................69
Question 59: Unable to delete companies...........................70
Question 60: Currency Converter tab: Online currency converter tool...71
Question 61: Project Contract Item Consumption Pricing....72
Question 62: Shared application tree between non clustered AOS...73
Question 63: Securing data through record-level security....74
Question 64: Route for costing 75
Question 65: Zero $ assets.......................................76
Question 66: Error when running some reports from the AOT 77
Question 67: AOS does not start....................................78
Question 68: Posting VAT during packing slip updating 79

Question 69: Allocation in Axapta Applications.................80
Question 70: Marking and Pegging in Axapta Applications. .81
Question 71: Operations Scheduling.................82
Question 72: Financial Statement creation.................83
Question 73: Two clients with and without KR1 on same PC 83
Question 74: Error Account.................84
Question 75: Financial Statement.................84
Question 76: Do update production costing more than once?
.................85
Question 77: Planned order fields 87
Question 78: No lines for posting or quantity 87
Question 79: Combination cost price.................88
Question 80: Capacity load on work center.................89

Axapta Database.................90

Question 81: Most efficient SQL statement - join order.........91
Question 82: Upgrading to AX4.................92
Question 83: SQL2005 & Axapta 3.0.................92
Question 84: AOS connection management.................93
Question 85: Connection to MSSQL database.................94
Question 86: Query to temporary table returns empty.........95
Question 87: Database Server size.................97
Question 88: Inventory in Axapta Database.................98
Question 89: Highest version of Oracle for Axapta 2.5 SP1. .98
Question 90: Axapta Purchase Orders.................99
Question 91: Axapta Compilation Errors.................100

Axapta Localization.................101

Question 92: Kanji in Axapta Localization.................102
Question 93: Brazilian localization.................102
Question 94: Deferred Tax.................103
Question 95: SP4 DIS layer for Western Europe.................103

Axapta Programming.................104

Question 96: Opening the external website 105
Question 97: Replace one field value with another.................106
Question 98: Button Hotkeys.................107
Question 99: Faster export to Excel.................108
Question 100: Passing multiple parameters to a lookup form
.................109
Question 101: Dynamic Grid Label 110
Question 102: Changing EDT Type.................111
Question 103: Use of the InventSumDelta table 112
Question 104: Get Fields from DataSource.................113
Question 105: Problem with Code Migration.................114

Question 106: List Box multi-select BaseEnum...............115
Question 107: Collection class Map.........................117
Question 108: Missing labels in X++........................118
Question 109: Supplementary items...........................118
Question 110: Limit on free text of 1000 characters...........119
Question 111: Select report design based on DataAreaId.....120
Question 112: TextIO <> AsciiIO 121
Question 113: Excel COM Export Performance...................122
Question 114: Batch journals across multiple companies....124
Question 115: Call debugger from X++ code....................125
Question 116: Form Tree Control - Display drag-over nodes
....126
Question 117: Exit after SysStartupCMD...................127
Question 118: WMS - Reduced Picks.(and Close)..............128
Question 119: Importing XPO Error.........................129
Question 120: Use of maps, still confused..............130
Question 121: Write method of data source is called
repeatedly...131
Question 122: OR ing in addRange()....................132
Question 123: Output data from different companies.........133
Question 124: Opening Form in Maximized mode...............135
Question 125: Variable declaration X++ versus CLR?........136
Question 126: EP-Standard WEBGRID & its Header Label.137
Question 127: Getting sessionId or workspaceId.................139
Question 128: Read file from directory...................140
Question 129: Using DataAreaID as a Table Index.............141
Question 130: Filter Button....................................142
Question 131: AX4 debugger missing values..................142
Question 132: Grid Label.......................................143
Question 133: FormTreeControl - FormTreeIt..................144
Question 134: Searching for specific EDTs...................145
Question 135: infolog.viewUpdate, write to top in Axapta
Programming..147
Question 136: Deactivate auto-complete.....................148
Question 137: Be interactive with a form or dialog through
X++ code...149
Question 138: Delete all data in a temporary table.............151
Question 139: Programmable Section......................151
Question 140: Select a record based on TableID and RecID152
Question 141: Clicking on grid makes form to appear 154
Question 142: NET Enums in X++...........................155
Question 143: Update data source..........................156
Question 144: Best way to get a table ID..................156
Question 145: Duplex Printing..............................157

Question 146: Display method name or path on an error message in exception handle............................158
Question 147: Prevent deletion of Invoiced Sales Orders....160
Question 148: Strange error in changing BOMConsistOf form 160
Question 149: Dynamic access to titlefield1.........................161
Question 150: Edit info text on top of EPSalesTableCreate. 163
Question 151: Inner select.......................164
Question 152: Grid DataMethod............................165
Question 153: Lexical Error.................167
Question 154: About Axapta reports...................167
Question 155: Importing Labels............................168
Question 156: To access application directory runtime.......168
Question 157: Problems updating a ProjJournalTable record 169
Question 158: Accessing Checkboxes..................170
Question 159: Save a file with the help of a SaveDialog........171
Question 160: ListIterator problem in 3T.............172
Question 161: End of file.....................174
Question 162: EDT Crash.....................175
Question 163: To retrieve the field(s) range on a form........176
Question 164: Users Online.................177
Question 165: Getting meta-information for menu items....178
Question 166: Get the application/environment from X++ 180
Question 167: Changes in tables........................180
Question 168: parameter character of num2str function.....181
Question 169: Multi-table Quotation report........................182
Question 170: Web portal problems..................184
Index...............................185

Introduction

Microsoft Dynamics AX is Microsoft's flagship enterprise resource planning software system. It is part of the Microsoft Dynamics family.

It was originally developed by Damgaard Data A/S as Axapta in Denmark before Damgaard was merged with Navision Software A/S in 2000. The combined company, initially NavisionDamgaard, later Navision A/S, was then ultimately acquired by the Microsoft Corporation in the summer of 2002. Before the merge, Axapta was initially released in March, 1998 in the Danish and U.S. markets. Today, it is available and supported in forty-five languages in most of the world.

Custom AX development and modification is done with its own IDE MorphX that contains various tools such as a debugger, code analyzer, and query interface. This development environment resides in the same client application that a normal day-to-day user would access thus allowing development to take place on any instance of the client. The development language used in Axapta is X++.

On June 9, 2006, Microsoft completed developing the latest version (4.0) in facilities spanning the globe and including sites in Vedbæk, Denmark; Kiev, Ukraine; Fargo, North Dakota, USA; and Redmond, Washington, USA.

MorphX and X++

MorphX is an integrated development environment in Microsoft Dynamics AX that allows developers to graphically design data types, base enumerations, tables, queries, forms, menus and reports. MorphX supports drag and drop and is very intuitive. It also allows access to any application classes that are available in the application, by launching the X++ code editor.

Because MorphX uses referencing to link objects together, changes in for example data types of fieldnames will automatically be reflected in places they are used (such as forms or reports). Furthermore, changes made through MorphX will be reflected in the application immediately after compilation.

Microsoft Dynamics AX also offer support for version control systems (VCS) integrated with the IDE, allowing collaboration in development. There is also a tool for reverse-engineering table structures and class structures to Vision.

Axapta General Discussion

Question 1: Visual SourceSafe and MDAX 4.0

I have installed Visual SourceSafe version 6 sp6. I want to use it inside AX. When I use the development tools version control - setup system settings and add a database, I receive this error:

```
"COM object of class 'SourceDepot.SDConnection' could
not be created. Ensure that the object has been
properly registered on computer 'WMLI009230'".
```

If I then use version control - setup - Version control parameters and change the Version control system to Visual Source Safe I receive this error:

```
"Cannot create instance of CLSID_VSSDatabase. Check
that Visual SourceSafe client is installed properly".
```

Do you have any solution to this problem?

A: Yes, there is a solution. You need to use VSS 2005.

Question 2: Sub-contract in AX4

I've been looking at the new sub-contracting processes in AX 4 for vendor production. This is where a company supplies raw material to a sub-contractor and in a single operation the sub-contractor makes a finished product or sub-assembly.

I can get the sub-contractor's route operation updated when I post a purchase order delivery note onto the related sub-contract purchase order. After which I get it to post a route card journal onto that operation, but I still have to post a report as finished journal (or update report as finished) on the production order. Normally, when you post a route card journal you have the option of posting report as finished if you're updating the last operation.

Is there a setup I need to do to accomplish this?

A: Unfortunately, it is currently not possible to use automatic report as finished feature when posting a purchase order from sub-contractor. It simply follows same rules as for the rest of automatic journal postings.

Automatic report as finished parameter is always copied from Production parameters to the header of route card journal, but copied to the journal lines only when a user manually enter the lines. That is the common rule for route card journal.

Question 3: ABC Codes

I am doing data conversion for the item form. There is a field
called ABC codes (Items form- others tab). Now, these item
codes have values None, A, B, and C. I don't know what these
stand for. I also checked the base enums but they all say just A,
B, and C under the properties field.

I have to update the ABC codes for something called "fast pick
items" which I guess is a customized value.

Can you give an idea what this particular value is for?

A: ABC is a classification of your inventory based on sales. You
have a few different categories in which to rank the items too.

Here is an example from my company:

The A items account for the top 80% of sales performance, B is
15% and C is 5%. Some items may be ranked high on the revenue
scale (A), but margin could be lower (B or C), which would
represent an item that we don't get great margin on, but sell
quite a bit of.

I hope the example makes it a bit clearer to grasp.

Question 4: User Admin is not connected to employee

I am getting the following error when I click on HR > Journal > Absence > Request.

"User admin is not connected to employee"

What does it mean? What do I do from here?

A: You need to check Administration menu > Users > select Admin user > User relations (button) and finally relate the user to an employee (General tab).

Question 5: Axapta Object Server 4.0 not restarting

We have single test server AXTST for Ax 40sp1 with 2 AOS installation and 2 Application files and SQL server 2005 on it with 2 AX databases. We have plans for restarting AXTST every Sunday at 03:50:00 after midnight. But after restarting the server on AOS, server 02 restarted automatically but 2nd server did not restart automatically. I got these error messages instead:

```
Time: 04:07:11
Source: MSSQL$SQL2005
Type: FailureAud
Event ID: 18456
User NT AUTHORITY\SYSTEM
Computer: AXTST
Descriptiption:
Login failed for user 'NT AUTHORITY\SYSTEM'. [CLIENT:
<local machine>]


Time: 04:07:11
Source: Report Server Windows
Type: Error
Event ID: 107
User: N\A
Computer: AXTST
Descriptiption:
Report Server Windows Service (SQL2005) cannot
connect to the report server database.


Time: 04:07:12
Source: MSSQL$SQL2005
Type: FailureAud
Event ID: 18456
User NT AUTHORITY\NETWORK SERVICE
Computer: AXTST
Descriptiption:
Login failed for user 'NT AUTHORITY\NETWORK SERVICE'.
[CLIENT: 10.1.2.11]


Time: 04:07:12
Source: Dynamics Server 01
```

Type: Error
Event ID: 140
User N\A
Computer: AXTST
Descriptiption:
Object Server 01: Fatal SQL condition during login.
Error message:
"[Microsoft][ODBC SQL Server Driver][SQL
Server]Cannot open database
"Demo5Ax40" requested by the login. The login failed.

Time: 04:07:12
Source: Dynamics Server 01
Type: Error
Event ID: 163
User N\A
Computer: AXTST
Descriptiption:
Object Server 01: SQL diagnostics: [Microsoft][ODBC
SQL Server Driver][SQL
Server]Cannot open database "Demo5Ax40" requested by
the login. The login
failed.. Connect information was: Userid = [],
Database = [Demo5Ax40], Server
= [AXTST\SQL2005], DSN = [], Other = []

Time: 04:07:12
Source: Dynamics Server 01
Type: Information
Event ID: 110
User N\A
Computer: AXTST
Descriptiption:
Object Server 01: Server main session is being
destroyed.

Time: 04:07:12
Source: Dynamics Server 01
Type: Information
Event ID: 108
User N\A
Computer: AXTST
Descriptiption:
Object Server 01: Dynamics Server has been stopped

Can you give some tips on how to deal with this?

A: Try a delayed service restart after the reboot (net stop/net start). It is most probable that the SQL is not accessible in current time.

Question 6: Reporting Server Role for AX 4.0

I am installing the AX Reporting Server Role, and I have to specify the source database. I have several databases (development, testing, UAT, training) and I want to be able to use them all.

Do I have to install the role on four separate servers?

A: There is no need to install the role on separate servers. If you look in Administration > Setup > Business analysis > Reporting services, you will see on the advanced tab, SSRS options AX report folder (defaults to Dynamics) and data source name (defaults to Dynamics Database).

The installer, when you specify the source database, creates the Dynamics Database data source that will contain "data source= SQL server you specified; initial catalog=AX database you specified".

You can use as many AX databases as you like from a single reporting server, but you have to set up the different AX report folder names and the data source name in each AX environment. You can then create these folders and data sources on the reporting server. Use the ones created by install as a template and you are set to go.

Question 7: Enterprise Portal Error message

I have two Windows 2003 standard server with the latest updates under one domain. The first server SQLDB01 has SQL server 2000 with sp4 installed and Axapta database. The 2nd server AXSRV01 has Axapta server and I have two installations on it with Ax 3.0 sp4.

I now want to install the enterprise portal on the server. But when I tried to install at the SQL server SQLDB01 and change the Identity to local administrator and to TEST in Axapta, I got this error message:

```
"The Microsoft Axapta Business Connector was loaded
without problems.
Could not logon to Microsoft Axapta.

This may be due to wrong or unspecified user name and
password for COM-logon in Axconfig.axc, or
permissions to the COM-logon do not exist.

Error information

Method 'logon2' in COM object of class
'AxaptaComConnector.Axapta2' returned
error code 0x80004005 (E_FAIL) which means :
Microsoft Axapta Error : An illegal directory
structure for Axapta has been detected.
The sub-directory V:\Axapta Application SP4\\bin does
not exist. Please restart the Axapta Business
Connector before logging on.

"V:\" is shared Directory for Application on the
AXSRV01 server.
```

Then I tried to register Enterprise Portal at Axapta server AXSRV01 then "identity" to local Administrator. I got this error message instead:

```
"The Microsoft Axapta Business Connector was loaded
without problems.
Could not logon to Microsoft Axapta
```

```
This may be due to wrong or unspecified user name and
the password for COM-logon
in Axconfig.axc, or that permissions to the COM-logon
do not exist.

Error information

Method 'logon2' in COM object of class
'AxaptaComConnector.Axapta2' returned Error code
0x80004005 (E_FAIL) which means : SQL error : SQL has
reported the following error:
[Microsoft][ODBC SQL Server Driver][Shared Memory]SQL
Server does not exist or access denied.. Connect
information was: Userid = [bmssa], Database =
[AXDB],
Server = [WMSI002561E], DSN = [], Other = [] You may
refer to the error log file for further details.
Retry the operation?
Please restart the Microsoft Axapta Business
Connector before logging on.
```

On both servers, the Administrator has the same password.

Can you tell me what might have caused the problem?

A: You need to use a domain user account to use the .NET Business Connector. A local administrator account will not do. Check the implementation guide for more information.

Question 8: Can't find Rapid Configuration Toolkit (RCT) anymore

The RCT download site somehow disappeared from PartnerSource. I know it was there because I just saw it the other day.

Do you know where I can get it?

A: Yes. Try visiting this site to download:

https://mbs.microsoft.com/partnersource/newsevents/news/newsgeneral/ax4orct.htm?printpage=false

Question 9: Microsoft.Dynamics.BusinessConnecto rNet.Axapta in BatchRuns

I am successfully using the Microsoft.Dynamics.BusinessConnectorNet.AxaptaClassLibrary to connect several independent AX-Installations. Now I am trying to work with BatchRuns to have my Systems connected.

Although I am using <<InterOpPermission.assert();>> the Logon Method of my Axapta-Object does not work at all.

The BatchQue and the BatchJob are running under my User Id, so I don't see any User Rights problem.

Is it a known bug, that the dotNet -Connector cannot be used in BatchRuns?

Do you have any ideas on how to deal with this sort of problem?

A: Class BatchRun is instantiated on the server. You will need to check your properties settings.

Question 10: Active Directory import wizard

I installed Dynamics AX 4.0 for evaluation. I am now trying to add a user importing users from the Active Directory.

The user Id was not filled out. When I tried to fill out the user Id manually I noticed that the next button is not enabled. It is enabled only for users with a user ID filled out.

Is there another way to add users?

A: Yes, there is. You need to add the user id and check the 'select' checkbox; then the 'Next' button should become enabled.

Question 11: AX4 SP 1 Location wizard

I'm trying to create locations in a warehouse (in the usual Aisle-Rack-Shelf sequence), but the Wizard only creates Aisles. I don't know if I'm missing something or the wizard is broken in AX4.

Can you help me out?

A: I don't think anything's wrong with the wizard.

In the warehouse, look for tab Location names. For instance, Rack, Level and Bin/Position should be switched on. Then the wizard will create locations as well.

Question 12: Delete BOM records

Is it possible to delete bill of material records using the excel import/export tool?

If not, what would be my best option?

A: Your best option would be to use the SQL table browser or SQL code to delete the BOM.

Question 13: Changing the language in Axapta 4.0

How can we change the language in Axapta 4.0?

A: You can change the default language by a user in the Tools/Options/Language and change the language. Your option is limited to the languages that you have purchased - under the language tab in the License information.

You have to close and re-open AX for the language change to take effect.

The default language codes (for sending out invoices, etc.) are setup under the Company information in the 'Other tab'.

Question 14: 4.0 SP1 User session no longer valid

I've recently upgraded a 3.0 SP4 Application to a 4.0 SP1. Everything went fine, but when users (or me, the Admin user) try to post a Purchase Order or a Sales Order or any type of document doesn't matter, this message is displayed:

"Your Microsoft Dynamics AX user session is no longer valid. Logoff your computer and logon again. If the problem persists, contact your Microsoft Dynamics administrator.

Tracing code shows that error appears in Formletter.dialog() method, not always in same line code."

Can you help me with this?

A: You will need to verify if you have Windows Server 2003 hot fix 913184 for the Remote Procedure Call engine. If you don't have it, you need to get it to fix your problem.

Question 15: Invite multiple attendees in MDY AX CRM-module

Do you know how to invite multiple attendees for an activity in the CRM-module of AX when these attendees are not fellow employees?

A: Yes. It is possible to do this in AX 4.0 where you press the attendees' button on the activities form and add attendees by adding records. The only field required is the attendees' e-mail addresses.

In AX3.0 and earlier versions, it is not possible. The attendees' functionality is primarily a quick way of generating activities for your co-workers.

Question 16: Synchronizing Data-Dictionary-ERROR

On which tables does synchronization have the highest probability of failing?

Error message is as follows:

```
"Error Synchronize cannot execute a data definition
language command on ().
The SQL database has issued an error.
Error Synchronize cannot execute a data definition
language command on ().
The SQL database has issued an error.
Error Synchronize cannot execute a data definition
language command on ().
The SQL database has issued an error.
Error Synchronize Problems during SQL data dictionary
synchronization.
The operation failed.
Info Synchronize failed on 3 table(s)"
```

Can you enlighten me concerning this matter?

A: Yes, definitely. On the SQL administration form, verify the Check / Synchronize option under Table actions is activated. This should fix the error message that you got.

Question 17: Maintenance Strategy

We recently went live with Axapta 3.0 and feel the need to develop a strategy for maintaining our data.

What is considered the best practices for data maintenance? When and how often do you perform the following?

-Re-indexing
-Consistency Checks
-Synchronization
-Database Log Cleanup
-Performance Analysis

Plus, are there any other tasks deemed important to properly maintain the database?

A: These are the standard maintenance strategy:

> Re-indexing
This is done once a year after end of year activities.

> Consistency Checks
It is a good practice to run checks after you set up new static data, for instance customers, items, routes, etc.

> Synchronization
This is needed only when upgrading the data structure; for instance tables or EDTs.

> Database Log Cleanup
There must be some reason why you are logging and what. You should determine this issue according to your company security policy.

> Performance Analysis
This is done the first time when you go live and then once a year after end of year activities and re-indexing.

Meanwhile, other tasks deemed important to proper database maintenance include the following:

- Watch that your backups do not fill the data or log disk.
- Take backups also from the document directories.
- Run SQL trace on selected users to find long running queries.
- Monitor reloading time and count of records of entire table cached tables.

Question 18: Rename AOS instance

I installed 2 instances of AX40 in one computer.

Can I rename one of the instances?

Or do I have to uninstall the instance first, then reinstall and assign the new name?

A: You have to uninstall the instance and reinstall it with the new name. AOS in AX 4.0 is now a service and services cannot be renamed.

Question 19: Deploying webparts on a Sharepoint site

I tried to deploy webparts to an existing Sharepoint portal site. I can select the vital web parts, but I don't get dynamic AX properties. I need to select the active company.

Is this a bug or did I miss something?

A: You need to register the site in AX. That should fix the problem.

Also, make sure the Business Connector is setup properly.

Question 20: Warning: Application Event Viewer

What does this warning mean? It appears whenever I start the AOS.

Detected SQL Protocol 's' is not recommended for Multi Session Navision Axapta use.

I am using Axapta 3.0 with sp5 connecting to a MS SQL Server 2005 Database with sp1 + kernel rollup 3.

A: The warning may mean that AOS has detected that you have enabled several protocols in the database server. The message normally occurs when you add the Named Pipes protocol to your protocol list.

When running Axapta against SQL, you should only have applied TCP/IP. The message will not lead to any errors in the way Axapta works and perform.

To resolve the issue, run SQL Server Network Utility and SQL Server Client Network Utility. Open the General tab and disable all protocols except TCP/IP. Most probably, you will disable Named Pipes protocol.

Here's what you need to do step by step:

1. Click Start, click Run, type cliconfg in the Open box, and then click OK.
2. Verify that TCP/IP is enabled and is the only protocol in the Enabled Protocols by order box.
3. If TCP/IP is not enabled, follow these steps:
    3.1. In the Disabled Protocols list, click TCP/IP.
    3.2. Click Enable to move TCP/IP to the Enabled Protocols by order box.
    3.3. Click Apply.

Question 21: Unable to create an Enterprise Portal

I have installed Dynamics Ax 4.0 (AOS on one server, DB on another server and .NET Business Connector + client on a 3rd server). This 3rd server has IIS and Sharepoint Services 2 SP 2 and .NET framework 2.

My problem is that I'm unable to create an Enterprise Portal from Sharepoint. I created a new site in Sharepoint, chose the Enterprise Portal Template and selected the DMO Company. The site is created but it doesn't show anything. When I look in the Event Log, I see this message:

```
-------------------------------
Web session initialization for Microsoft Dynamics
failed.

CryptoAPI not available.
CryptoAPI not available.
Error executing code: CryptoAPI object not
initialized.

Stack trace

(C)\Classes\CryptoAPI\salt
(C)\Classes\WebSession\clientCryptoInitializationVect
or - line 10
(C)\Classes\WebSession\parseArgs - line 93
(C)\Classes\WebSession\init - line 17


Microsoft.Dynamics.BusinessConnectorNet.BusinessConne
ctorException
at
Microsoft.Dynamics.BusinessConnectorNet.AxaptaObject.
Call(String
methodName, Object[] paramList)
at
Microsoft.Dynamics.WebParts.SessionCache.SessionItem.
Microsoft.Dynamics.WebParts.ISession.InitWeb(HttpCont
ext context, Boolean isPostBack)
-------------------------------
```

I have tried to investigate this from AX, but the CryptoAPI class is a system class.

Can you point me where to proceed from here?

A: You need to check that the logon alias for the Business Connector Proxy account has been setup correctly. Go to Administration\Setup\Security and open the Business Connector Proxy form. The account in the form should match the account under which the Application pool on the IIS box running the Business Connector is started.

In addition if you want to disable URL encryption in EP you can do so on the Parameters form in Administraton\Setup\Internet\Enterprise Portal. Make sure Enable Encryption is not checked.

Question 22: Importing BOMs from Excel

Is there something I need to setup to import BOMs and BOM lines?

I created an Excel template from the Template Wizard including the BOM, BOMTable, BOMVersion, and BOMConfigRoute tables. I filled out the information box in the BOM, BOMTable, and BOMVersion tabs in the spreadsheet. I was told to include the BOMConfigRoute table as well, but not sure what to fill out in that tab in the spreadsheet. After importing the spreadsheet, the BOM and version are created, but with no lines in the BOM Lines form. The BOM line data exists in the table in the AOT.

Is there something that I missed in the setup for the data similar to specifying the Dimension No. in the InventItemLocation and the three entries in the InventTableModule for item imports?

A: If you can see the records in the table browser after an import but not on the form, then probably the reason is an invalid (or blank) InventDimId. Each BOM line can specify a warehouse; that's what the InventDimId is doing.

Another data load tip is to create a record manually, and then carefully compare a record created by the data load with the manual record, field by field, using the table browser. It shouldn't take you long to identify the problem.

Question 23: Sync error in AX4.0

When synchronizing in Dynamics AX, I get this SQL error:

```
"Cannot execute a data definition language command on
(). The SQL database has issued an error.
Problems during SQL data dictionary synchronization.
The operation failed.  Synchronize failed on 1
table(s)".
```

My problem is how to find the table where the sync error occurs. In Axapta 3.0 the table name was mentioned in the error message.

How can I fix this?

A: You must use the server configuration utility and check the client tracing checkbox on the Tracing tab for the AOS instance. Then you will get the error message you expect.

Question 24: KR2/KR3 Installation

I have yet to install kernel rollups and would like some advice on installing KR2 and KR3. We are currently on 3.0 SP 2 KR1 and need to go to at least KR2 if not beyond.

Is it recommended to go to KR2 first then to KR3 or is it fine to go directly to KR3 from KR1?

A: KR3 does not support 3.0 SP2, but KR2 does. So you must upgrade to KR2. Make sure to read the document 'KR2 Readme.doc' included in the upgrade package.

Question 25: AIF

We are trying to create a sales order using AIF. We created a console application and added the web reference as per the instruction provided by Microsoft at:

https://mbs.microsoft.com/partnersource/documentation/samp ledata/ax4odemodata

We are using default web service created during installation of AIS.

When we tried to run this console application, it gives the following error:

```
The description for Event ID ( 0 ) in Source
( Dynamics Application
Integration Server ) cannot be found. The local
computer may not have the
necessary registry information or message DLL files
to display messages from
a remote computer. You may be able to use the
/AUXSOURCE= flag to retrieve
this description; see Help and Support for details.
The following information
is part of the event: An error occurred while Web
service request
http://localhost/DynamicsWebService/SalesOrderService
.asmx and action
createSalesOrder were being processed. Error details:
AifRequestProcessor-processInbound Request Failed.
See the Exception Log for
details..

**Exception:**

Message: AifRequestProcessor-processInbound Request
Failed. See the
Exception Log for details.Stack trace: at
Microsoft.Dynamics.BusinessConnectorNet.Axapta.CallSt
aticClassMethod(String
className, String methodName, Object[] paramList)
at
Microsoft.Dynamics.IntegrationFramework.WebService.In
tegrationProcessor.SubmitMessage(String aifMessage).
```

How do I fix this problem?

A: You need to check in your .Net Console App that the message header part is defined properly, for example, Context EndPoint, Destination EndPoint, UserId and Password, etc.

You can also go to Basic -> AIF -> Periodic -> Exceptions to see exactly what error is being logged.

Question 26: Removing an Enterprise Portal Site Documentation

Page 177 of this document (Document 8621X_AX40_WN_TECH.pdf Version: AX-Dynamics 4.0/Win 2003/MS-SQL) says:

To remove a site association:

Click ADMINISTRATION->SETUP->INTERNET_ENTERPRISE PORTAL->ENTERPRISE PORTAL

I find no second reference in the Administration, Internet menu for Enterprise Portal, therefore the next reference pertains to:

In the Virtual server URL list, select the server you want to remove Enterprise Portal from, and then click Remove.

What is the correct "click through" to obtain and remove an Enterprise Portal Site or Association from a location?

A: You can remove it via:

Administration --> Setup --> Internet --> Enterprise Portal --> Manage Deployments

Here you can find the virtual server list and the described button 'Remove'.

Question 27: Remove accents from strings

I'm French and I'm an Axapta developer. I need to remove accents from strings for export, before I send them to a text file, which will be opened by an external application that crashes with accented texts.

I haven't found a standard function to remove the accent. When I do, for example, replace ("é","e") that doesn't work, Axapta does not see the difference between é and e.

I have thought that maybe an upper case could remove the accents but I'm not sure and I haven't found the function to do this.

Can you help me?

A: Most probably, your problem is a standard function strReplace:

```
static str strReplace(str _str, str _fromStr, str
_toStr)
{
int charNum;
int fromLength = strLen(_fromStr);
int toLength = strLen(_toStr);

if (_fromStr != _toStr) // <== is true for eg. é and
e
{
...
```

If you comment this "if" statement or use your own function and not checking _fromStr and _toStr, the replace function would work just fine.

Question 28: Best Practice Checks meaning

We transferred our add-ons to Ax4 and are cleaning up our best practice errors.

Can you explain the following best practice violations to me?

TwC: Validate access to return value from display/edit method
TwC: Validate data displayed in form is fetched using record level security.
Dangerous API FormListItem used."
TwC: Assert usage of API COM.Zoom because it is protected by Code Access Security.

A: It is good for you to actively clean up your best practice errors. The errors starting with TWC are all Trust-Worthy Computing related.

I suggest you start out by reading our whitepaper "Writing Secure X++ Code".

Question 29: VendPaymProposal, find a specific spectrans

For each ledger journal transaction, there can be several spectrans. In the VendPaymProposal form, the datasource on the grid is ledgerjournaltrans. The same record is shown for each instance of a spectrans, because of the join.

But if I delete one of the spectrans (delete the line in the grid where my cursor is), the cursor goes to the first 'line' of the ledgerjournaltrans, from which I delete a spectrans. I need to know which spectrans is the next, so I can somehow get the cursor to the 'line' that is shown for the spectrans that comes after the one I deleted.

Can you give any ideas on how to do this?

A: In the AX3.0 versions, you can't do what you are asking. There are some technical issues which show how the form is designed in 3.0 and will do what you would like to transpire.

If it is any comfort, this is fixed with the new payment proposal in 4.0.

Question 30: Close All Open Forms

Is there a shortcut key that will close all open forms?

The "Esc" closes one form at a time but I want to know if there is a key combination that will close, for example, 10 open forms.

A: Yes, there is a shortcut combination of keys. You can use the Menu Bar WINDOWS>>CLOSE ALL; keyboard shortcut would be Alt+W+A.

Question 31: Take out AX4.0 Find filter (Ctrl-K) pre-populated text

We recently upgraded our Axapta from AX3.0 to AX4.0. The Find filter in the new version has the text box pre-populated. We would like to take the text out so that the user does not have to delete it before the users' inputs the find criterion.

Do you know a solution for this?

A: You will need to update with SP1.

As I understand, the searching tools should then be X++ enabled, so you can manipulate them through X++ code.

Question 32: Active Directory Import

When I start the AD Import I can see all AD Users but only some of them have a UserID entry, and only these are importable.

How can I add a UserID for the others?

A: As far as I know, only users with network names up to 5 characters have their user id pre-filled. Longer names don't, because user id in AX has a maximum of 5 characters only. You must enter user ids for such users manually.

Question 33: Duplicate qualifications not allowed in Axapta HR

There appears to be a validation rule or something that's preventing users from entering more than one type of qualification in the employee table within Axapta HR. For example, if you try to enter BA (Bachelor's degree) in English then BA in Math, it won't allow the BA in Math because there are two instances of the same type of qualification.

Is this a 'standard / out of the box' functionality in Axapta?

Can you give any suggestions about how this problem can be fixed?

A: Yes, this is standard behavior. This is due to the fact that the index on the table does not allow duplicates. Basically, you cannot perform the skill-mapping if you have multiple educations with the same id.

You need to set up individual educations, for example "BAEng" and "BAMath", in the HRMEducationType form. If you wish to group all the BA educations together, then you set up an Education Group called "BA" in the HRMEducationGroup form and attach it to the education.

Question 34: AX4.0: Database transfer

Goal: Transfer an AX4.0 DB from a customer site to a partner site (on 2 different Windows Domains) without having to recreate a full AD structure.

I would like to know if there is an alternative to the following procedures:

- Full SQL DB backup from the customer
- Full SQL DB restore on the partner SQL server
- From SQL Management Studio, modify table USERINFO, find record with ID 'Admin', and modify NETWORKALIAS, NETWORKDOMAIN and SID with the corresponding info from the logged-on user.

A: As far as I know, editing the userinfo table is the only way to do this.

Question 35: Authentication problems

I am trying to set up Axapta 4.0 web sites for my company but keep running into problems I do not understand. I think I have installed everything by the book. The problems occur when I try to create a new website and add site templates to it.

To create a new top level site in SharePoint Central Management works fine, but when I connect to the newly created site to add site templates, a login window with username and password pops up. This is not expected, but I still typed in the domain name\administrator username and password. This user owns the sites. After typing this three times I get the message that I am not authorized to view the site. I also don't reach the site by registering the site in Axapta. The Website also works slowly when this happens.

I have managed to reach the register site window once with a different site, and this site seems to communicate with Axapta. This is when I am giving users in AD/Axapta access to enterprise portal. But with this site, I experienced the same problem when I tried to watch the website with the users I have granted rights to watch the EP AX site. I suspected this problem to have the same origin as the one above.

I have all the components on one server for test purposes. I will use two servers when I implement it for real. So Windows 2003Srv (AD), AX AOS and Client, MSSQL2005 ISS and Windows Sharepoint Service are running on the same machine. I also tried remotely connecting to the server and open a browser there but I still get the same problems.

I have also verified that I have the right versions of all the components and that ISS is set up with integrated windows authentication.

Do any of you have a clue about what is wrong with my system?

A: You can start by checking the following.

Do you get the same authentication error when you try to create any standard WSS site such as Team site? If that happens, then it could be your IE settings. Try to add the site to the trusted site in IE.

Are you using NTLM authentication or Kerberos? When you extend the virtual server you can set the authentication type. Set NTLM for EP.

Make sure the APP Pool account used by IIS is a domain account and configured in AX as Business Connector proxy account.

Question 36: Axapta 3 to AX 4 upgrade documentation

I have prepared a copy of my production environment which I plan to upgrade to AX 4 as a test. What I have not really encountered is what are the steps in the upgrade? I think it's best for me to have a little more know how before proceeding.

Can you suggest any materials that can help a lot?

A: Yes. You can search AxImpGuide with the phrase "Flowchart: Upgrade Methodology".

Question 37: Overlap time

Do you know what the meaning of "Overlap time" of an operation is?

A: Actually it is called "Overlap quantity", and the meaning of which I would like to explain with the following example.

Assume you have a production order for 100 pieces and it has two operations, 10 and 20. Normally operation 20 will start only after entire quantity (100 pieces) has been processed on operation 10, BUT when you have specified something in "Overlap quantity" field, let's say 5 pieces, it means the next operation (in our case 20) can already start when only 5 pieces has been processed on the operation 10.

In Dynamics AX 4.0, "Overlap quantity" parameter is made to be calculated. It is done during the estimation of production order in order to prevent situations where the second operation is faster than the first one and when overlap is used, it might finish earlier than the first one, so the calculation of optimal overlap quantity is made and compared with the one entered.

Also a new field 'Transfer batch' is introduced to specify in what batches finished goods should be moved between operations; it is used in the overlap calculation.

Question 38: Production costing, Inventory closing

I have a couple of questions:

1) A Picking List Journal (and its lines) is created automatically if one selected the 'Complete picking list journal' flag in the 'General' tab during update to 'Start'. One can then enter consumption per line. Is there a way to automatically populate the 'Consumption' field to values equal to the 'Proposal' field when the lines are generated?

If this could be accomplished, one need to only update consumption to specific lines that needs changing. Since this becomes very important when dealing with BOMs that can have many, many lines, perhaps there's another way of handling this.

2) Would it be possible to run Inventory Closing for one item group, or at least for one specific warehouse?

There are three 'Specification' options in the 'Closing/Adjustment' form but apparently the selections serve other purposes that are not clear to me. I saw that it is possible to do a 'Recalculation' for an item or an item group but 'Adjustments' require "at least one closing" according to the online help in AX.

A: The answers are numbered accordingly.

1) Normally, when you start a production order and automatically create a picking list journal, the Proposal quantity is copied to the Consumption field and there is only one case when it is not (when the item in picking list has 'Release' parameter marked), you can find it in Inventory management -> Items -> References -> Production group -> Release.

2) Unfortunately, it is not possible to run Inventory closing for the item group or warehouse or any other selections. It is done for an entire inventory. But as you noticed, 'Recalculation' will work for it.

Question 39: Production costing

I set up a typical 'work order' with suborders and tried to advance the production through all phases. My interest was to be able to see the realized consumption and cost of a sub-production/work order before the main order is completed. I posted material consumption using the 'Picking List', and checked to see if I can see actual material consumption on the 'Price calculation' window. However, both the 'Realized consumption' and 'Realized cost' fields remain blank. I then advanced the sub production all the way to 'Costing' including updating an 'End' Reported as finished but still the 'Price calculation' window does not update with the actual realized quantities.

I even ran the production costing report but that came up as empty as well.

Can you help me reach the realized consumption vis-a-vis the estimated consumption?

A: I assumed you are using Axapta 3.0. In AX3.0, realized costs are calculated only during Costing phase. There are number of parameters specifying whether calculation should be done or not.

Please make sure parameter Production -> Setup -> Parameters -> General -> Estimation -> Price calculation is marked.

Also check parameter Production -> Production orders -> BOM -> General -> Calculation; it should be set if the component must be included in the calculation.

To include job times (setup, process) to the calculation, you need to check Route group attached to the production operation and set required parameters under "Estimation and costing" section.

In Dynamics AX 4.0 costing process is improved and you can already see realized prices after posting of production journals (picking list, route or job cards), without waiting until production order is cost accounted.

Question 40: Text file to be generated via Axapta

Can you guide me how to create a run time text file to a selected folder through Axapta, if this text file already exists in the designated folder for example, BatchText1.txt?

It should create a new file with a new number BatchText2.txt, and so on.

A: You can use this example:

```
static void Job1(Args _args)
{
Filename filename;
;

filename = "c:\\temp\\BatchText1.txt";

if (WinAPI::fileExists(filename) == true)
{
filename = fileNameNext(filename);
}

WinAPI::createFile(filename);
}

fileNameNext is a method in class Global.
```

Question 41: SQL 2005 Enterprise Client Required for Axapta v3 AOS environment

I would like to know if our customer is required to have SQL 2005 Enterprise Client if they are installing Axapta V3 in AOS environment.

Can you give a good recommendation?

A: If they are running version 3.0 of Axapta, SQL 2000 will work fine as the database engine. SQL 2005 is only supported on Axapta 3.0 if the minimum install is service pack 2 and a kernel rollup (currently KR2) is applied. KR2 allows the database to run in 'native' compatibility mode.

Please note that if this is a new installation, SQL 2005 needs to be run with SQL Authentication (mixed mode); the database and bmssa user will have to be created manually.

Question 42: Forecast Consumption in Axapta

I am looking for a setup that allows Axapta planning to consume forecast by actual sales in a specified period. There is a setting on the master plan to allow reduction of forecast by open sales orders, but I also need to be able to reduce it by closed sales orders that are shipped within a specified period.

Can you give any ideas on this?

A: The setting says "Open orders" but it works for sales orders that are shipped in a given period. You can try this test.

Setup monthly forecasts and run master planning. Setup a sales order due to ship next month. Run master planning. From this point, you can now ship the sales order. It will net off against this month's forecast.

Question 43: AX 4.0: no more aoc-files?

Can you tell if the Axapta Object Cache files (*.aoc) still exists?

I can not find anything on my AX 4.0 client. If they are still used, has anything changed compared to previous versions concerning:

- naming conventions of those files and
- preconfigured master.aoc

A: The extension for those files has changed to .auc (AX User Cache) and is now located in:

C:\Documents and Settings\<win_username>\Local Settings\Application Data\

Question 44: Dedicated link from AOS to SQL DB

Both my AOS & MS SQL server have 2 NIC, AOS -191.168.1.1 & 131.1.1.1, MS SQL-191.168.1.2 & 131.1.1.2. The 191.168.1.x is connected to my switch while 131.1.1.x is connected between AOS & MS SQL servers using cross-cable.

The intention is to speed up data transfer. But I notice that there are activities only on the 191.168.1.x connection even though I can 'ping' through 131.1.1.x.

Is there a way to set which NIC/IP to use when AOS communicate with MS SQL?

191.168.1.x is my LAN IP for all PCs.

A: The AOS is listening only to the first NIC, as seen in the even viewer. This NIC should be connected to the LAN side while the other NIC of the AOS is connected to the AOS and application.

You can change the logical order of the NICs in the Control panel -> Network -> Advanced settings.

Question 45: Kernel Rollup - Best Practice

I have read a lot of threads regarding KR1 and KR2. I am a bit confused about the practice on this subject. As I have understood, KR1 is primarily updating Axapta to support SQL Server 2005 and update AOS. Is that correct?

What about KR2? Is it primarily a "patch/problem solver" for the kernel, or the reason for updating another?

Generally, is Kernel Rollup part of the so-called "Best Practice"?

A: To elucidate the issues you mentioned. I would say KR1 performs the following:

• Compatible with SQL Server 2005
• Performs Optimistic Concurrency Checking for SQL Server 2000 and SQL Server 2005
• Enhance Axapta SQL Server Tracing Utilities
• Increase SQL Query Performance
• AOS Enhanced Stability and Logging
• AOS Abort if Listener Thread Fails
• Enhanced Password Security (application update required)

Meanwhile, KR2 does the following:

• AOS/COM Connector Stabilization fixes
• Enhanced PDF Functionality
• SQL 2005 Stabilization
• Oracle Upgrade Stabilization
• Setup Changes for KR2
• Help/TechNet link updated to Axapta Community Site

I highly recommend you install these 2 KRs as they improve the system on some important technical points.

Question 46: Multi-channel order processing

I would like to know if Axapta is capable of handling mail-order processing.

Besides mail orders, does it support orders placed through the Web?

A: Yes, it does. You can configure the enterprise portal customer role in order to enter orders via the web.

Question 47: AOS licenses

I am configuring an educational environment in three-tier. Our students become programmers/system developers. For this purpose we have licenses for all the modules and the development environment in Axapta 3.0. We have licenses for one AOS and none AOS-Add-On users.

The problem is I can not log on the AOS with a client, but I can start the AOS.

Do we need licenses for some AOS-add-on users?

A: You do not need the AOS Add-On Users license if you have an 'Enterprise' Base Package. That license key was used for an old license model for a "small" Axapta.

There must be a problem with your client-authentication.

Question 48: ActiveX Error in Application Object Tree

We have a situation where the creation of a Gantt chart in AX 3.0 is not working from a Terminal Services client session but is working from RDP to the SQL server.

I first thought this was another table permissions issue, but now I don't think so. Both sessions are logged in as the same user. In the Application Object Tree the Gantt chart is an ActiveX control.

Could it be that something needs to be enabled or installed on the TS to enable ActiveX controls?

A: When you are using Gantt chart within Dynamics AX, XGantt ActiveX must be registered in the operation system where AX client is installed. XGantt ActiveX includes following files which have to be located in the same place or folder:

vcgantt.ocx
vcwin32.dll
vcpane32.dll
vcprct32.dll
vxcsv32.dll

In order to register XGantt ActiveX, you can run: "regsvr32 vcgantt.ocx".

Question 49: Migration to V4 from V3 SP4

I am running a code upgrade as described in the help files of Dynamics AX 4.0, and therefore, I copied all high layers from V3 to V4 application folder.

Now, due to the number of custom codes, I have a lot of conflicts with the new version. So I use the compare tool to check which conflicts I should solve.

Among the custom code, there are a lot of code lines that look like:

```
// AX SP3 Addition
... some code here...
// AX SP3 Addition
```

I wanted to make sure that all code additions from service packs are natively included in AX v4, so that I will never have to add the few SP lines into the new custom V4.

Are all SP issues up to SP5 corrected in V4?

A: Corrections applied to older versions are included in the current version. I am not sure, if all corrections of 3.0 SP5 are included in AX 4.0, but they will be in 4.0SP1 for sure.

Do not try to correct Microsoft code that was changed or added in AX 3.0SPx for version 4.0. There are some design-changes made and code cleanups, so you might miss some comments like those you stated.

If you upgrade from one version to another, just keep your changes made to the standard code and re-implement them in the new version. The challenge is to keep the delta you have applied to the old version, since this is the added value of your custom installation.

Question 50: AX Team Server Setup Installation Error

When I attempt to install Dynamics AX Team Server, I get the following error:

'Setup requires the .Net security level for this zone to be set to full trust. The security level can be set from the .NET Framework Configuration
in Control Panel.'

I first cannot figure out which 'zone' it is referring to but I have set all zones to full trust but the installation still will not start. I set the all Zones to Full Trust through the .NET Framework Configuration in Administrative Tools.

Can you help me with this?

A: The fix for this problem is simple. Just copy the TeamServerSetup.exe to a local drive.

Axapta Applications

Question 51: Delete Ended Production orders

Is there a way to prevent ended production order from being deleted?

A: There is no specific parameter for that, but it can easily be done via code. Just add the method below to the class ProdStatusType_Completed.

Code:
```
boolean validateDelete()
{
    return checkFailed("@SYS18511");
}
```

Question 52: Axapta Batch Server Installation

How do you install an Axapta Batch Server?

I know it must be a Three (3) tier client but that is about all the information I can get.

A: As far as I understand, an Axapta batch server is simply an Axapta client running a batch queue server process from Main menu \Basic \Periodic \Periodic \Batch \Processing.

Question 53: AX and NAV

What's the difference between NAV and AX?

Are NAV and AX 2 different ERPs?

How do they complement each other?

A: Both are ERPs and under the same MS Dynamics umbrella. However, AX supports more number of concurrent users and is now in mid market segment companies, but NAV caters to a very low number of concurrent users and is for very small companies or workshops.

Question 54: Automatic Processing of Sales Orders

Is there anyway to setup automatic processing of Sales Orders in AX?

I assume that there should be a way of using the batch processing. However, I can't figure out how to make it process the new sales orders. What I can do now is select one or more sales orders, select Confirmation or Invoicing, and it will process those orders accordingly and automatically.

What I'd like to be able to do is have orders created within AX and if an order exists that has a Document Status lower than 'Confirmation', then the Confirmation batch would pick that sales order up and confirm it. Likewise I want it to do the same thing for orders that have a status of 'Packing Slip' that has not been invoiced. Surely every company running AX that has large numbers of sales orders doesn't have someone sitting in front of a console manually selecting orders and confirming them and invoicing them on a daily basis.

A: Yes, you can set up each of the postings to be run by a batch process. From the Main Menu, go to Accounts Receivable > Periodic > Sales Update > *Update of your choice*. This opens the SalesEditLines form just like it would for posting a single sales order. Use the select button to set up the criteria for orders you wish to post and use the Batch button in the bottom right to set up a schedule for it.

A word of caution though. If you set up the query to pick up orders with a status < Confirmation, it might be possible that an order would be grabbed in the middle of a salesperson entering in lines.

Question 55: Ax 4.0: Usage of OLD folder

I have installed an AX 4.0 application. I am wondering if there should be any OLD folder under the "..\Microsoft Dynamics > AX\40\Application\Appl\Standard" path.

The purpose is to use the compare function in AX, but then I need a folder to place old *.AOD files.

A: It's actually an oversight on the installation. The folder was never created. You can create one there yourself and name it "Old".

Question 56: Set up of Transfer Orders in 4.01

Can you guide me on the setup and use of the new Transfer orders functionality in AX4.0?

I've been trying to post a shipment for a transfer order between two of the warehouses and I keep getting this error:

"Inventory dimension Location must be specified."

I already set up a transfer warehouse for these two warehouses. It has a single aisle and location. I specified this location as the default for receipt and issue for the transfer warehouse. I also set up a breakpoint during execution and it's failing the check in the method \\Classes\InventMovement\checkDimPhysical on the line:

```
if ( (this.dimSearch().dimPrimaryStocking()) ||
(_qty > 0 && !
this.dimAllowBlankReceipt(this.dimSearch())) ||
(_qty < 0 && !
this.dimAllowBlankIssue(this.dimSearch())) )
```

Am I missing a setup step?

A: You need to set up locations on your transit warehouse for inbound and outbound docks. Then you can assign these locations to the warehouse's default receipt and issue location on the Warehouse Management tab.

Question 57: Project and type Fixed-Price

I am new in using Project and cannot find where I should state the sales price for a project type Fixed-Price. The sales price should also be the income for the project.

Can you point me to the right direction?

A: The sales price or revenue from a fixed price project comes from an account transaction Project/Projects/Button: Invoice/On account where you can then enter the installments to be paid by the customer.

Question 58: Error creating production journal

We have been getting a sporadic error message when trying to create production journals. The message states than it cannot create a journal because journal number 384427 already exists. Currently our production journals are in the 4176XX range, so it is referencing a 6+month old journal. The user will close out the message and the form and try it several times. After a while it succeeds creating a new one. While the error is happening, we have checked for locks, but didn't find any.

What can be causing this type of issue?

A: You sometimes get this type of error when the number sequence is set to 'Continuous' and the number that exists finds its way into the list of numbers that the system tries to re-use. If you don't need the numbers to be continuous, switch that off; otherwise, delete the number from the missing list.

Question 59: Unable to delete companies

I have run into a problem in trying to delete a company in AX 4.0. While I was creating the company (as a duplicate of another company), the process erred out because of a problem between the schema in the AOT and the schema in the database.

This issue with the schema has been fixed but I am not able to delete the company. When I attempted to delete it, I got the following error message:

```
'Error Message (11:56:27) User 'mk' is not authorized
to delete a record in table
'SYSPERIMETERNETWORKPARAMS'. Request den
Error Message (11:56:27) Cannot edit a record in
Perimeter Network
Parameters (SysPerimeterNetworkParams).
Access Denied: You do not have sufficient
authorization to modify data in database.'
```

I think the cause is that the copy erred out before the security information can be copied. When I go into the company in question, I can't access anything.

What can I do to be able to delete this company?

A: Unfortunately, this is a known issue with Dynamics AX 4.0 RTM. The problem is that the company did not get added to a domain which is the last step in creating a company because of the error.

This has been fixed in SP1 where the transactions for creating the company and adding the company to the domain have been combined to prevent this from happening.

Try to manually add the copied company to any existing domain. If that succeeds, you should be able to delete the company.

Also, disable a validation check in the company form to allow you to add the company to the domain.

Question 60: Currency Converter tab: Online currency converter tool

I am using AX 4.0. Under General Ledger > Setup > Exchange Rates, there is a tab called "Currency Converter". At the top of this tab it says "Online currency converter tool".

What exactly does this do?

A: With the "Online currency converter tool" you can display converted amounts for amounts in company currency. For example if your company currency is in USD and you want to see the USD amount in GBP you can use this tool.

You must double click the currency code in the right corner of the AX status bar to select the currency you want to show your amounts in.

Question 61: Project Contract Item Consumption Pricing

We have an AX 4.0 project-based client who sets up project contract specific sales pricing on materials consumed on a time and materials project. They do not "stock" consumed goods, but merely purchase service items directly to the project. The PO is created from the Project and contains the project information, including the item category attached to that transaction. The pricing that comes through to the project, is the price set for the item in the item master.

What we need is to be able to set up pricing rates that are project specific. Is there a way to do this in standard AX that we have overlooked?

If not, can this be accomplished with a third-party or customization?

A: This is at Projects/Item tasks/Item requirement. The fields that you are interested in are all there although the layout may need work for efficient use. Use Functions/Create purchase order to create the PO. Look at project Sales orders to see the sales pricing. When the PO is delivered 'Consume to the project right away' and this delivers the item to the project.

Invoice in the usual way choosing Delivered sales orders.

Question 62: Shared application tree between non clustered AOS

What are the risks when I use one (1) application tree for separate non clustered AOS'?

Every AOS has its own database. I know that the online users are not working correctly, but can this also have impact on my caching, etc. I know that Axapta is not designed to be used this way.

Can you kindly give comments on this?

A: If you do not modify the application, there should not be any problems.

However, if you try to modify the application especially the Data Dictionary and try importing projects, you will have a lot of problems with DB for sure.

Question 63: Securing data through record-level security

I understand that security keys provide display/edit/delete/full access to menus, tables and fields. I also understand that record-level security is used to control access to data that is shown on forms and reports.

Can record-level security be used to show data on forms and what data can be edited on the forms as well?

For example, on the Item master if I set record-level security to display only those items in item group MAINT this works fine. Then, when I try to create an item in an item group other than MAINT, such as TEST, I am allowed to create the item. I can not view what I created because the record-level security is only allowing me to see items in MAINT, but I can still create the item in a different item group.

Is there any way to prevent this or is record-level security for display-only purposes?

A: I don't think that Record Level Security on the Item Master would achieve 'edit/create' restriction. However, if you create another Record Level Security entry for Item Groups table, then the restricted Item Group would not be visible in the drop down on the Item record although there is still no restriction on manually typing in the 'restricted' item group id.

Question 64: Route for costing

In Axapta 4.0, can we configure that a route be used for costing purposes only and not use for capacity planning? For example, the route will be used for bom calculation and production costing only.

I do not use the route setup time or run time to calculate the MRP date. Instead, I want Axapta to use the "Inventory lead time" for MRP planning time calculation.

A: The standard way to do this is by setting the parameters of the Routing Group set on the work center/route operations so that the operation is included in cost calculations but not included in capacity calculations.

Question 65: Zero $ assets

We would like to track assets from the fixed asset sub ledger that is below the scope of our capitalization limit. For example, our IT group would like to track the serial number, asset tag number, support contract info for all the laptops we purchase. In doing so, we do not capitalize the first letter of the words. Another issue I am facing is we cannot add zero $ assets.

Can you suggest any solution for this?

A: I presume the reason why you want to add "zero" assets is because you don't want them to have any impact on your P&L and Balance Sheet.

In this case you could create a new Value Model and set up the Posting Profile so this new Value Model uses a single ledger account (e.g. the error account) for all the different transaction types. If someone creates transactions on a fixed asset with this new value model, you'll get a debit and a credit transaction on your error account that cancels the financial effect.

It doesn't matter what value you "acquire" the assets at; you could use 0.01 because of the posting setup. Also, it may be a good idea to deselect the "depreciation" flag on the Value Model so that Dynamics AX does not include these assets in the depreciation run.

Just be aware that if you follow this setup, you'll not be able to sell a "zero" asset through a Free Text Invoice or a Fixed Asset Journal. If you choose to do so anyway, you'll have an imbalance on the error account or whatever account you chose.

Question 66: Error when running some reports from the AOT

Why is an error generated when attempting to run some reports from the AOT?

For example, when I attempt to 'Open' the BOMCalcTrans report in the AOT, I get the error:

```
'Error executing code: BOMReport_CalcTrans object not
initialized.

Stack trace:
(C)\Classes\BOMReport_CalcTrans\parmInventDimParm
(D)\Reports\BOMClacTrans\Methods\init'
```

I have made a copy of this report that I would like to enhance but I am unable to run either one from the AOT.

Is it possible to write a job order to perform this?

A: It is difficult to say why this isn't working for you without seeing the entire query/data source. I can't see from what you wrote if you have joined the InventTable and BOMCalcTable datasources. Both would be required.

In this case I think creating a new display method on BOMCalcTable to get the item name would be much easier for you to do. The method can look something like this:

```
display ItemName itemName()
{
;
return InventTable::find(this.ItemId).itemName();
}
```

You can drag the new display method from the AOT into your report.

Question 67: AOS does not start

We are educating programmers/system developers. During the education, we have an Axapta programming course. In that respect, I am about to setup an Axapta environment for my students, and I would like to setup a three (3)-tier environment. Until now, we have run the course in a two (2) - tier environment.

According to the help system in Axapta, it should not be a problem at all. Just set up and run a 2-tier first and then install the AOS. There are no service packs available yet. But every time I start the AOS, it shuts down shortly afterwards.

How do I resolve this problem?

A: Check your windows event log. It might be that the port is already in use, or the server can not connect to the database or that it cannot access the application. But I am sure that the event viewer will tell you a little bit more.

Question 68: Posting VAT during packing slip updating

I am trying to set up posting physical sales tax in connection with updating of packing slip to the General ledger. I already set up the Inventory parameters (Post physical sales tax), Inventory models groups (Post physical inventory), Accounts payable parameters (Post packing slip ledger) and also Inventory posting for Packing slip tax on the Purchase order tab.

When I update the packing slip, there are transactions on the general ledger, but no transaction for VAT is reflected.

How can I figure this out?

A: Looking inside the code, I've found that this part is related to the periodic form "Physical Posting" (Inventory Management > Periodic > Physical Posting). From this form, you can click the "Post" button, select some option and run it. I had to close the "Physical Posting" form and reopen it to see the result.

This is the only place in the code where the "Post Physical Sales Tax" and "Post estimates periodically" are used. They are not in the PO post packing slip.

Question 69: Allocation in Axapta Applications

How and where do I setup Firm/Hard or Soft Allocations in Axapta?

A: Allocations are initially 'soft', that is, reservations against a quantity per inventory dimension. For example - by warehouse. Stock can be successfully reserved if there is sufficient quantity per the inventory dimension. At this stage, no reference is made to actual stock receipts, unless the inventory dimensions include serial/batch control.

Allocations become 'hard' when the stock is picked. Reference is then made to an actual physical inventory receipt.

Marking can be used to specifically convert a reservation (soft) to an actual inventory receipt (hard).

Question 70: Marking and Pegging in Axapta Applications

Is there any relationship between Inventory > Marking, and Master planning coverage as seen in the Pegging panel in the Item > Inquiries > Net requirements form?

I created a few sales order lines, and production orders, and used Inventory > Marking from the production orders to link the production orders to the sales order lines. Then I ran the master scheduling and looked at the Pegging.

In SP5 it seemed that the 'Pegging' followed the 'Marking', but in SP3 it didn't.

Should it be that way? If not, why does master planning ignore the marking?

A: The pegging should follow the marking. I had a quick look at the code and there is no difference between SP3 and SP5. If the inventory transaction for the issue has a reference lot, a receipt with a matching Lot Id is searched to cover this issue. There is just one deviation from this; if the receipt was received, then there will be of course no receipt record and the issue can be settled against an on hand record.

Question 71: Operations Scheduling

When using operations scheduling, how do I rearrange a part of the schedule?

For example, if I want to bump a job ahead and no capacity is available for the work center, how do I make it go to the head of the list? We use production orders with references to sub-productions.

A: Have you tried re-scheduling the production order? Just schedule it forward from today, or forwards from a scheduling date. For example, indicate the start date you want.

If you don't select finite capacity scheduling, you should be able to insert the production order in the job queue wherever you want. But this schedules the whole production order. I don't know of any way to schedule a single operation.

Question 72: Financial Statement creation

I have a problem when I create a financial report. I would like the system to retrieve an accumulated amount. This is the field you can see when you go to GL > Chart of accounts > Period balances button.

How can I create a financial statement?

In columns, I already check 'include opening'. Are there other settings I need to do?

A: Make sure you have the appropriate date intervals (GL > Setup> Periods) set up.

Question 73: Two clients with and without KR1 on same PC

We just applied KR1 only to our test system. For about a month, I want to be able to login to test (KR1) and 'go Live' (without KR1) both from my PC.

Is there a way to do this?

A: Yes, there is. First, make a backup of your client folder before you install the KR1. Use the exe in that folder to connect to an application without KR1. Use the upgraded exe to connect to KR1.

Question 74: Error Account

May I know how Axapta's System Error Account works and in what condition this account will be posted?

A: Axapta's System Error Account works when the system encounters errors while posting vouchers.

An example: You import a G/L journal with some G/L chart of accounts that does not exist. When you post, some vouchers gets posted to the 'error account'.

Question 75: Financial Statement

I have a problem when I create a financial statement. I have one (1) formula line that comes from minus 2 total lines. For Example:

C = A - B, A is Gross profit, B is Total expenses.

How should I write the report?

Can you give suggestions on how to do it best?

A: Create your C column type = calculation and then click on calculation tab and enter your A & B into the formula accordingly.

Question 76: Do update production costing more than once?

Is it possible to update production costing more than once?

My company applies the standard cost method for FG item. We set standard cost price for each item since first creating the item and we never change it.

Now the auditor asked us to change the standard cost to become the previous actual cost from production. We know that we have to update costing for all the production orders that are already reported as finish but we still have some order which we intend to continue in the production after costing.

We're not sure what the right practice is. Can we continue the production further, pick RM after the first costing and update costing the second time?

A: Partial costing is possible but not recommended. A possible problem with this is that Axapta will put all current costs on the items that went through costing.

Consider the following example:

You have a production order for 100 pieces. There is a route with three operations, two of which are finished for all 100 pieces. You consumed all of your material (for 100 pieces), because maybe it is consumed with the first operation.

For the third and final operation, 50 pieces are finished.

If you do a costing now, those 50 pieces will bear the material cost for all 100 pieces and the labor costs for all 100 pieces for operation 1 and 2, beside the labor cost for operation three.

At this point in time you'll have a way too high on hand value for this item.

After you finish your remaining quantity of 50 and need to do a costing again, Axapta will fix this as well as the 50 pieces that went through costing first. But if you sold the first 50 pieces already, this sales order will have a wrong cost price, and must be fixed by doing a recalculation or inventory closing.

Question 77: Planned order fields

Can SchedToDate and ReqDateDlv of ReqPo have different values and when?

A: A planned order has a delivery date (calculated from its lead time and/or scheduling) and a required date (calculated from the demand). If the delivery date is after the required date, then you're going to be late, and you will see future messages.

Question 78: No lines for posting or quantity

I have a couple of users who are getting "no lines for posting or quantity=0" errors when trying to post POs in Axapta 3.0. The POs do have lines, and those lines have quantities. Another user, whose Axapta privileges are identical, can post the same PO without incident.

Can you give any clue as to why this happens?

A: Check the 'Quantity' drop list in posting form. Looks like one of your users is picking up a default of 'Deliver now' or something in that line; they should be using 'All'.

Question 79: Combination cost price

Can you explain the function of "use combination cost price" tick in item table?

A: Of course. The combination cost price allows you to have different standard cost price per each size or color for example. Standard cost price can be specified per item in items form on Price/Discount tab page. But here, you can specify common standard cost price for each sizes or colors. Combination cost price gives you possibility to have individual standard cost price for each color or size.

Question 80: Capacity load on work center

Is there a way to upload the capacity on a work center with report as finished journal if routing card is not posted?

We want to wait until the month finishes to post.

A: There are production parameters which control whether capacity reservations are updated by report as finished journals and route card journals. If you tick the update capacity on the report as finished journal, Axapta will only delete all the capacity reservation, and then only if you tick the report as finished 'end' flag.

I assume that you want to progressively update the outstanding capacity reservation based upon partial completions reported as finished. I think that only a route card journal can do that, so I suggest that you use update > report as finished, and use automatic route consumption to create a route card journal automatically.

Axapta Database

Question 81: Most efficient SQL statement - join order

Multiple test scenarios could not explain if and what the most effective SQL statement should look like using Axapta on an oracle database.

We use 2 tables, A and B as example. A has criteria, B has the sort criteria. Is it best to:

"select A join to B" or
"select B join to A"

Is there a 'best practice' or optimal query in this case?

A: The answer is much more complicated than the question, because it depends on:

- How many rows do each table have?

- Are sorting order fields index-able?

- Are criteria fields index-able?

Only with the right amount of prepared data for each table can we tell the 'best practice' for your case.

Question 82: Upgrading to AX4

We are an SQL2000 shop running AX3, KR1. We will be upgrading toAX4 (at least on a test environment).

Do we use this as a time to upgrade our DB to SQL 2005 and are there improved end user monitoring tools in Ax4?

A: Regarding the eventual upgrade to SQL-server 2005; one point might be that neither Ax 3 nor Ax 4 can take advantage of the SQL server 2005 "native mode".

If you choose to upgrade to SQL server 2005, the engine operates in "SQL server 2000" mode. No immediate enhanced reporting functionality or performance tuning is required.

Question 83: SQL2005 & Axapta 3.0

We are now working with SQL2000 and Axapta 3.0 SP1.

When we want to upgrade to SQL2005, do we need to install SP5 for Axapta 3.0 or is the Kernel Rollup enough?

A: Kernel Rollup-1 requires a minimum of SP2, so you would at least need to get to that level.

Also, KR-1 is actually a higher build that SP5.

Question 84: AOS connection management

I like to know more about the way the AOS manage the SQL or Oracle connections.

First, I would like to know about the '1 per 3 tier' user connections.

Secondly, with a pool that has many connections simultaneously, how and when does the AOS increase or decrease the number of connections?

Can you give a brief explanation on these?

A: There are about 2 connections per each active user, one for browsing and another for updating. Axapta maintains non active connections in a pool because creating one takes too much time. If there are free connections in the pool, AOS uses them first even if they are needed by another user session. You can not know which physical client uses which connection.

AOS releases connections when they are not needed. With SQL-server the timeout defaults to 1 minute and with Oracle it is 30 minutes. You can modify this setting in the AOS configuration utility.

Question 85: Connection to MSSQL database

In the axconfig tool it is no longer necessary to enter a name for the database connection. At runtime, a connection is created to the database using the settings in axconfig.

However, it can only be used if the database accepts mixed access. If the database security is set to windows authentication, I still have to use an ODBC connection.

Is there a way to work around this?

A: I don't think it's possible. In an ODBC configuration, you're able to specify that you want to login with your network login ID. In your Axapta configuration it's only possible to specify a database user and nothing for you network login ID.

Question 86: Query to temporary table returns empty

I can not retrieve the records from a temporary table using the Axapta's query class. Here is a code example:

```
void reportQueryBuild() // Method from Class MyClass
{
tmpSalesAnalysis tmpSa;
SalesAnalysisView sa;
QueryBuildDataSource qbds;
QueryRun qr;
Query q;

;

q = new Query();
qbds = q.addDataSource(tmpSa.TableId);
//tableNum(tmpSalesAnalysis));

while select sa order by AccountNum, itemId,
dateFinancial
where sa.DateFinancial
{
tmpSa.CustAccount = lastSa.AccountNum;
tmpSa.CustName = lastSa.CustomerName;
.....
tmpSa.insert();
}

//qbds = q.addDataSource(tmpSa.Data().tableId()); //
nothing works

qr = new QueryRun(qbds);

// this loop never run, besides tmpSa has more than
10 000 records
while (qr.next())
{
sa = qr.get(tableNum(tmpSalesAnalysis));
print sa.accountNum;
pause;
}
}
```

Can you help me locate the problem?

A: You will need to add just one line code before the while loop and it should work.

```
qr.setCursor(tmpSalesAnalysis);

// this loop never run, besides tmpSa has more than
10 000 records
> while (qr.next())
> {
> sa = qr.get(tableNum(tmpSalesAnalysis));
> print sa.accountNum;
> pause;
> }
> }
```

Question 87: Database Server size

We are converting a new client from SAP who is used to needing a very large database which is over 100G. They are worried that 200G isn't going to be enough space for the dedicated SQL Server. I can't seem to find any information on total capacity recommendations for the database server.

Can you give any suggestion or recommendation concerning this matter?

A: Based on the information provided, I think that you will be fine for storage. Please note that this is not a guarantee, just my personal opinion.

The biggest concern is using document handling. I am not sure about the amount of files that you are talking about or what type of enterprise portal customers that you are talking about either. However, there is an easy solution: create two file types. One file types the files that are stored in the database; these will be the files that users of the enterprise portal that are not internal employees need access to. The second file group will point to a network folder that is accessible to users. Simply specify the file type when importing the documents.

Question 88: Inventory in Axapta Database

Is there a way that I can get an on hand report for the past two (2) months for the inventory?

A: Yes, there is. Check out inventory -> reports -> status -> physical inventory.

Question 89: Highest version of Oracle for Axapta 2.5 SP1

What version is the highest that Axapta 2.5 with Service Pack 1 will be compatible with?

We are planning to upgrade Oracle to version 9.2.0.x with this version of Axapta.

Is this possible?

A: As far as I know Axapta 2.5 has never been tested on Oracle 9.2.0.x and therefore would not be supported. This is especially true since the Axapta install is only SP1. For Axapta 2.5 SP2, Oracle 9.0.1 is the highest version listed as supported. I could not find a listing for SP1.

Question 90: Axapta Purchase Orders

If an item is already registered in a purchase order, is there a way of reversing this?

A: The same screen in which you register can reverse the registration as long as stock postings have not been made.

After registering the PO line, select stock/registration and click auto against the line you want to cancel; this will create a reverse registration.

If it won't let you, then the stock may have been physically updated.

Question 91: Axapta Compilation Errors

I tried to setup a demo installation of Axapta. When I came to the Installation check list and I click on the Compile Application, I got the following error message:

```
Error in file: C:\ .....Location...\Axapta
Application\appl\standard\axapd.aoi while change to
write-acess in record=0
File id...:1
Windows error:=
Error code: 13 = Permission denied
```

I used SQL Server 2000 with SP3 and Axapta 3.0.

Can you give an explanation as to why the error occurs?

A: It is a security issue. Make sure you checked write access on the folder.

Axapta Localization

Question 92: Kanji in Axapta Localization

Does Dynamics AX support Kanji?

A: Dynamic AX 4.0 is Unicode. It supports Kanji characters.

Question 93: Brazilian localization

One of our customers is working with Axapta 3.0 SP4. They also have another business unit in Brazil.

I would like to know if the Brazilian Localizations are available for Axapta 3.0 SP4.

A: The Brazilian localization is available for Axapta 3.0, but in SP5 version. You can have access to it through partnersource.

Question 94: Deferred Tax

Is it possible to configure in some cases to create the invoice, register the tax in a bridge account, when payment is made to settle the invoice, and the tax amount will be transferred from the bridge account to the final tax account?

A: Yes, it is possible using two (2) sales tax codes and linking them with the field "Payment sales tax code" only for the first sales tax code.

Post an invoice using the 1st sales tax code, and the settlement of the payment with the invoice will move the Tax from the first sales tax code to the second.

Question 95: SP4 DIS layer for Western Europe

Do you know if there is already a Western Europe DIS layer for Ax3 SP4 available?

PartnerSource doesn't seem to carry it.

A: Try to log to Navision Partner guide/ Global systems / Product download / your country /Navision Axapta.

Axapta Programming

Question 96: Opening the external website

I need to open an external website from a menu item to be located on the main menu.

What's the best way to achieve this?

As an example, a menu item that will open the web browser and go to, say, http://www.microsoft.com.

A: The easiest is to create a job (or class), and write the single-like code in it.

```
static void Job41(Args _args)
{
;
WinApi::shellExecute("http://www.microsoft.com");
}
```

Then, point the Menu Item to this job (or class).

Question 97: Replace one field value with another

I have a table, InventTable in which I need to replace the value of all the fields that have a value HairAppliance to HA.

I am sure I can use a job to do this but I'm not aware of the syntax.

Can you help me with this?

A: This is a basic example of a job on how to update records.

```
MyTable myTable;
;

ttsbegin;

while select forUpdate myTable
where myTable.Description == 'oldValue'
{
myTable.Description = 'newValue';
myTable.update();
}

ttscommit;
```

Question 98: Button Hotkeys

I am using Axapta 4, SP1. When I add new buttons to forms, I get a hotkey e.g. "Ok (B)" or "Ok (D)"
(Alt-B or Alt-D) associated with the button.

Is there a way to totally disable this shortcut?

A: I don't think you can turn off shortcut keys in general. But on the actual button, you can set the property 'ShowShortCut' to 'No', and then the shortcut for that key would be disabled.

Question 99: Faster export to Excel

I am exporting large amounts of data from AX3 to Excel with codes like:

```
COMappl = new COM(#Excel);
COMworkbooks = COMappl.workbooks();
COMworkbook = COMworkbooks.open(fileName);
COMworksheet = COMworkbook.activeSheet();
writing to individual cells like
COMrange = _COMworksheet.Range(strfmt("%1%2",
_excellCol, _excelrow));
COMInterior = COMrange.interior();
COMColor = COMInterior.Color(color);
COMrange.value2(value);
Endusers report that the export is slow.
```

Are there faster ways, classes or plug-ins I can use?

I remember doing the same exports from a Delphi 5.0 application, using some 3rd party plug-in and it was fast. I also need to color code individual cells.

A: It would need some coding but you can create XML file which can be read by Excel as xls file. You just need to produce flat XML file. It's fast.

Also, try to use ADO.

Question 100: Passing multiple parameters to a lookup form

I am currently calling a lookup form using the following code:

```
Args args = new Args();
FormRun FormRun;
;

args.name(formstr(ItemLookup));
args.parm(SalesLine.CustAccount);
args.caller(element);
FormRun = new FormRun(args);
FormRun.init();
this.performFormLookup(FormRun);
```

I would now like to pass more than one parameter to the lookup form.

Is there an easier way of doing this?

A: Yes, there is and here are three (3) of them:

1) You can form an object containing the needed values (List, Set, Array, etc.) and pass it in the parmObject method of args class.

2) You can create a method in the called form, that has the needed arguments list (or, container, for example), and call it after formRun.init();

3) You can create a method in the calling form, that returns the needed data (in a container, for example), and call it in the lookup form's init method.

Question 101: Dynamic Grid Label

I built a grid dynamically from a dictTable declared:

```
Grid_AJFull is grid,
Grid_AJFull.addDataField(SISAssignJnlFullTable_ds.id(
),
dictTable.fieldName2Id(assignJnlFullSetupTable.SISAss
ignJnlDynamicTypeName));
```

I want to change the label of the data field I just added, but I don't know how get to the controls.

Can you help me?

A: You can do something like this:

```
--------------------------------------------
void init()
{
FormStringControl newGridField;
;

...
Grid_AJFull.addDataField(SISAssignJnlFullTable_ds.id(
),
dictTable.fieldName2Id(assignJnlFullSetupTable.SISAss
ignJnlDynamicTypeName));

newGridField =
Grid_AJFull.controlNum(Grid_AJFull.controlCount());
newGridField.label("New label");
}
--------------------------------------------
```

Question 102: Changing EDT Type

I need to change an EDT and all its related fields from type int to string.

Can you think of a quick way of doing this without having to redefine everything?

A: Sorry, but I don't think this can be done the easy way.

The change means deleting not only info in AOD and some of the system tables, but also in the database. It's a whole lot of a change you have to do to change an EDT.

Question 103: Use of the InventSumDelta table

In trying to resolve a problem with a modification done to our AX3.0 system (reserving stock at the warehouse level instead of the location level), I have come across a problem with a table.

In class InventUpd_Reservation's updateReserveMore method, there is a Boolean value called mustIncludeInventSumDelta. If this gets set to true, it includes a join statement to the inventSum query that returns the quantity on hand available for reservation.

Without this join, the inventDim record for warehouse reservations is included in the inventSum query. When it is joined with InventSumDelta, the reservations made against the warehouse are not found.

What is the purpose behind InventSumDelta?

Can I ignore it safely in this case?

What criteria are used to determine if the flag "mustIncludeInventSumDelta" is set to true?

A: The purpose of the InventSumDelta table is to avoid locking on the InventSum table. During transaction all inventory movements will be recorded in the InventSumDelta table (i.e. when InventTrans is inserted or updated). When the transaction is to be committed, the method Application::ttsNotifyPreCommit is called and the contents of InventSumDelta are added to the relevant InventSum records. This replaces the IMTS in Ax 3.0.

This avoids locking InventSum until the very last moment.

You should use InventSumDelta whenever the on-hand may be changed in the same transaction as the calling code.

Question 104: Get Fields from DataSource

How can I get a value field from DataSource?

A: Here is a full example: (based on InventTable)

```
Common table;
;
info(strFmt("%1",
InventTable_ds.cursor().(fieldNum(InventTable,
ItemName))));
table = InventTable_ds.cursor();
table.(fieldName2Id(table.TableId,
identifierStr(ItemName))) =
InventTable.ItemName + "HELLO";
table.update();
```

Question 105: Problem with Code Migration

I tried to quickly move codes from Axapta v3 to AX4 SP1 and I encountered this problem: some classes does not exist any more in V4 and I can't find where to put the added code made in V3, for example, LedgerReport_ProvisionalBalance.

Do you know of a correspondence class list from V3 to V4 or something like that, and if there's none, what's the best and fastest way to find the new name of classes in V4?

A: In AX v3 many Ledger reports are using class which name is like LedgerReport_*. In V4 there is no more of those classes like you said and the class code (methods) is now in report.

For example the methods of LedgerReport_ProvisionalBalance class are now in report LedgerProvisionBalance.

Question 106: List Box multi-select BaseEnum

Is it possible to do multi-select on a BaseEnum on a form?

I was checking out the list box, but it seems that it can only select one item at a time.

I want to filter a grid based upon an enum, and let the user select multiple possibilities. So after searching, I wanted to loop through the selection and add query ranges.

How can I achieve this?

A: First of all, I think that using the standard filter button would be highly preferable. You can select multiple values there by using wildcards (separating the values with a comma, or a '..' , etc.)

The ListBox control doesn't allow selecting two items at a time. The ListView control does but it has to be filled from code.

Here is what you need to do. Create a List View control on the form. Insert the call to the following method before super() in the run() method.

```
void initListView()
{
SysDictEnum dictEnum = new
SysDictEnum(enumNum(StatusReceipt));
int idx;
str labelValue;
;
ListView.viewType(2);

ListView.singleSelection(NoYes::No);
ListView.checkBox(NoYes::Yes);

ListView.deleteAll();
ListView.addColumn(0, new
FormListColumn(dictEnum.label(), 0, -2));

for (idx = dictEnum.values() - 1; idx >= 0; idx--)
```

```
{
labelValue = dictEnum.index2Label(idx) ?
dictEnum.index2Label(idx) :
dictEnum.index2Symbol(idx);
ListView.addItem(new FormListItem(labelValue, 0,
dictEnum.index2Value(idx)));
}
}
```

This will build the ListView based on the BaseEnum that you will specify in the 3rd line.

You can multiselect, but I prefer the CheckBoxes as they are easier to grasp for the user.

Now, in order to form the QueryBuildRange, you have to use code like this one:

```
int idx;
str range;
FormListItem item;
;
super();

idx = ListView.getNextItem(FormListNext::All);
// idx =
ListView.getNextItem(FormListNext::Selected);
while (idx != -1)
{
item = ListView.getItem(idx);
if (item && item.stateChecked())
// if (item)
range = queryRangeConcat(range,
queryValue(item.data()));
// idx = ListView.getNextItem(FormListNext::Selected,
idx);
idx = ListView.getNextItem(FormListNext::All, idx);
}
box::info(range);
```

The commented lines are for the case with the Multi-Select option.

You may also want to check out the tutorial forms about ListViews (tutorial_form_ListControl and tutorial_form_ListControl_CheckBox)

Question 107: Collection class Map

I am using the collection class map to store some calculated figures per sales Id.

But I am experiencing some peculiarities when performing the calculation for all sales Id (65877 pieces); it seems that the value of some keys gets another value compared to when performing the calculation for say 4 sales Ids. Are there any limitations on a number of elements that one can use in a map?

A: No, there should not be any problems with 65000 keys in the map.

When the map is filled, output the number of elements in the map (map.elements() does this).

The amount of elements will be less than you expected; map.insert(key, value) replaces the values, if key is already in the map. You should choose the key type and values carefully so that they do not get overlaid or duplicated.

Here is a sample proving that a map can handle a large number of values (100000 in the example).

```
static void Job17(Args _args)
{
Map map = new Map(Types::Integer, Types::Integer);
int i;
MapIterator mi;
;
for (i = 1; i <= 100000; i++)
map.insert(i, i);

mi = new MapIterator(map);
mi.begin();
while (mi.more())
{
infolog.messageWin().addLine(int2str(mi.value()));

mi.next();
}
}
```

Question 108: Missing labels in X++

I am looking for a code routine using X++ that will help me identify labels used in X++ code that don't exist in the corresponding label file. Example: A label named "@AA123" is used in a table method. The label does not exist in label file "AA".

The routine should look into all methods of all objects and when it finds a label it would need to perform a search into the label file. If the label is not found then an info log would be displayed or a temporary table can be filled. I think I should be able to use the TreeNode class in conjunction with SysLabelFind class to do this but I don't know for sure. I would prefer to see a sample on the proper way to do this.

Can you suggest on how to do this?

A: Yes, there is a BP check for this.

Check method checkLabelBasics of class SysBPCheck.

Question 109: Supplementary items

In the salestable form, I like to open the supplementary items form automatically if a supplementary item exist.

Is there a way to determine if there is a supplementary item?

A: Yes, there is. Try using mst_pgv.

Question 110: Limit on free text of 1000 characters

Is there a limit on free text of 1000 characters?

Is it possible to expand it to 2000 characters?

A: The Free Text type is a Memo type EDT. So, the size of this EDT is limited only by your computer's memory amount.

Here is a test job that works correctly on my PC (the contents of test.txt is over 2400 characters).

```
static void TestFreeTxtType(Args _args)
{
FreeTxt f1, f2;
TextBuffer tb;
TextBuffer tb2;
;
tb = new TextBuffer();
tb.fromFile("c:\\test.txt");

print tb.size();

f1 = tb.getText();
print strLen(f1);

f2 = f1;
print strLen(f2);
tb2 = new TextBuffer();
tb2.setText(f2);

print tb2.size();
tb2.toFile('C:\\test2.txt');
pause;
}
```

Question 111: Select report design based on DataAreaId

I want to select a report design based on the DataAreaId of the used administration in Dynamics.

What method do I need to add to the report for this job to be done?

A: In order to select a specific design, you have to write a single line of code in the init method of your report:

```
this.design('TheDesignNameYouWantToSelect');
```

And in order to link this to a specific company, I would recommend creating a setting in the corresponding Parameters table (for example, CustParameters). The settings will be different in each company and you will just modify your ine of code this way:

```
this.design(CustParameters::find().MyReportDesignName
);
```

Question 112: TextIO <> AsciiIO

Can you differentiate TextIO and AsciiIO class in AX 4.0 SP1?

A: If you use TextIO you can specify a codepage. The default codepage argument -1 will correspond to files being written in Unicode format.

If you use AsciiIO, your files will always be encoded in ACP (Ansi Code Page).

Question 113: Excel COM Export Performance

I'm currently experimenting with the Excel COM interface, as I need a few exports directly into Excel. For a start, I know CSV and it is currently not an option. My current approach sets every cell individually using the widely published Cell.Value() semantics.

Since most of the time here is spent within Excel, I suspect that the huge numbers of individual COM calls are a bit of a problem here, I have been trying to reduce them. My current and only approach here is to use the range assignment operations of Excel, according to the Excel documentation. The code I tried looks roughly like this:

```
// Populate Values
excelWorksheet.range(strfmt('%1%2:%3%2',
'A', currentLineNumber,
'AA', currentLineNumber)).value(values);
```

Where values are an array holding a bunch of COMVariant objects fitting into the specified range. They consist of Strings, Ints, Dates and Reals.

I have taken this idea out of an Excel Automation help file I downloaded from technet, which states among else:

```
'Add headers to the worksheet on row 1.
Set xlSheet = xlBook.Worksheets(1)
xlSheet.Range(xlSheet.Cells(1,1),xlSheet.Cells(1,3)).
Value = Array("Order
ID", "Amount", "Tax")
```

Unfortunately, everything the COM Libs do here is to throw a rather general error code 0x80020005 which Axapta translates to DISP_E_TYPEMISMATCH.

Can you help me resolve this?

A: One example is shown below:

```
COM actSheet;
COM range;
Array arr;
...
while ()
{
...
arr = new Array(Types::String);
arr.value( 1, strfmt("%1", ledgerTrans.RecId));
arr.value( 2, strfmt("%1", ledgerTrans.AccountNum));
arr.value( 3, strfmt("%1", ledgerTable.AccountName));
arr.value( 4, strfmt("%1",
ledgerTable.AccountPlType));
arr.value( 5, strfmt("%1",
ledgerTrans.BondBatchTrans_RU));
arr.value( 6, strfmt("%1",
ledgerTrans.BondBatch_RU));
arr.value( 7, strfmt("%1", ledgerTrans.TransDate));
arr.value( 8, strfmt("%1", ledgerTrans.Txt));
arr.value( 9, strfmt("%1", ledgerTrans.AmountMST));
arr.value(10, strfmt("%1", ledgerTrans.Crediting));
range = actSheet.range(strfmt("A%1:J%1", row));
range.value2(COMVariant::createFromArray(arr));
```

Question 114: Batch journals across multiple companies

I have a series of batch jobs that are run daily. At the moment I have six (6) companies and run each batch job for each company.

Is there any way to run a batch job across multiple companies?

A: Yes, there is. In AOT there exists a table collection function termed 'Batch'. You can create a virtual company, which is based on that table collection and include all your company within this table.

After that you will be able to configure one batch server, which will serve all your companies.

Question 115: Call debugger from X++ code

Is it possible to call the debugger from X++ code without setting a breakpoint?

I am thinking of something like the code below:

```
---code above
if (condition == true)
{
//**** OPEN THE DEBUGGER IN THIS POINT ****//
}
---code below
```

A: Yes, it is possible to call the debugger. Try this:

```
---code above
if (condition == true)
{
breakpoint; //hardcodes a breakpoint into your code
}
---code below
```

Question 116: Form Tree Control - Display drag-over nodes

In the bomtreeDesigner you can select a node in the tree and drag it to another place. The nodes hit by mousepoint have a red line instead of the blue color. I tried looking into the code but can't find the solution.

What can I do to fix this problem?

A: It's the formTreeControl.setInsertMark. In your dragOver method, use:

```
FormDrag dragOver(FormControl _dragSource, FormDrag
_dragMode, int _x, int _y)
{

FormDrag formDrag = FormDrag::None;

[treeItemIdx] = this.hitTest(_x, _y);

formDrag = _dragMode;

formTreeControl.setInsertMark(treeItemIdx,true);
return formDrag;
}
```

And in your drop method, use the following:

```
formTreeControl.setInsertMark(0,true);
```

Question 117: Exit after SysStartupCMD

Can anyone tell me how to wait for a form/menuitem exit before I continue in the code?

I have created a new entry for SysStartupCMD, to start a Standard form. I call the form with:

```
MenuFunction::runCalled(.......
```

What I want is to exit when returning from the form.

Is there any way to wait for the form to exit before I continue in the code?

A: Yes there is. Try wait() method on FormRun object after call form.

Question 118: WMS - Reduced Picks.(and Close)

I am trying to reduce picking lines on a picking route. This works fine, but when it comes to generating a packing slip for this line, and chooses the CLOSE mark (leave rest pick), I get the following message:

```
"ordered qty cannot be reduced because there is not
enough invent transactions with status 'InOrder'.
Items are 'Sold','Deducted' or 'Picked'."
```

Do you know why the packingslip is being aborted?

The child reference for the inventTrans is WMSOrder, while the movement searches for 'blank' transactions (non existent for this InventtransId).

A: Once the inventtrans have the child reference set to WMSOrder, the WMS system has control of them. So in your scenario you only picked e.g 3 out of 5, which means that there are still 2 that are under WMS control. You need to end the output order to remove the childref, and then you can finish your scenario.

Question 119: Importing XPO Error

I never had this problem before, but now when I import my XPO onto stock AX I am getting the error message:

"Error: One or more arguments are invalid."

Do you know what causes this?

If I close the import screen and reopen it, then the XPO imports without any errors.

A: You need to put a breakpoint in class Info the add() method (Press F9 e.g. in the first line after the variable declarations in method Add()).

Try to import again to get the error message. This time the X++ debugger should appear, and the call stack will give some information about what goes wrong. For example, which function got an invalid argument, or which function called it, etc.

Question 120: Use of maps, still confused

I am not sure where and how we can use maps?

Can I use map to insert values in table?

A: Table maps are a kind of inheritance model for tables. For example, the AddressMap; a lot of tables have a common set of fields and methods for address data and these tables are related to the map.

This allows you to write code dealing with the address matters, not knowing if it is the address of a customer, vendor, SO etc.

Question 121: Write method of data source is called repeatedly

I have a form with two tabs. Each tab has a grid tied to a data source. When I enter a record in one grid that violates the primary key and click the other tab, the write method is called on the first data source to write that invalid record. It rejects the record and shows an error message. As soon as I try to click on the form to correct my error, the error message pops up again. While debugging, I see that the write method is called over and over again which is causing that error message to pop up over and over again. The error can be fixed if you move the infolog out of the way and go back to the other tab and remove the record, but it is not very convenient.

Is there a better way of handling this situation?

A: You can find a similar pattern on the InventTable form, between the InventTable datasource and the InventTableModule datasources.

Try to override the validateWrite method and check for the primary key violation there. Then return checkFailed ('some error message').

Question 122: OR ing in addRange()

I have the following method:

```
public void executeQuery()
{
QueryBuildDataSource qbds;
Query query;

;

query = this.query();
qbds = query.dataSourceNo(1);
qbds.clearRanges();

qbds.addRange(fieldnum(MyTransactions,SentBy)).value(
gCurrEmp);

//OR

qbds.addRange(fieldnum(MyTransactions,SentTo)).value(
gCurrEmp);

}
```

How do I achieve OR ing between this two (2) addRanges?

By default it gets And' ed.

A: Try using:

```
qbds.addRange(fieldnum(Cg_AwfTransactions,SentBy)).va
lue(strfmt ('((%1 ==
"%3") || (%2 == "%3"))', fieldStr(Cg_AwfTransactions,
SentBy),

fieldStr(Cg_AwfTransactions, SentTo),
gCurrEmp));
```

Question 123: Output data from different companies

We have to put some customer account data on an excel-file with a little job. So we took all data from all companies.

Is it possible to get the other companies' customer data, without making the table virtual?

A: This is from the developer's help (version 3.0).

When working with more than one company, use the following guide:

Large companies are often split up into several legal entities. MorphX supports this by using the changecompany function in X++.

The change company statement is used to alter the database settings to another (separate) company. The syntax of the statement is:

```
Changecompany = changecompany (expression) statement
```

The expression is a string expression, which defines which company is to be used.

The statement is executed on the new company. The example below shows how to use this statement.

```
static void main()
{
Custtable custtable;
;
// Assume that we are running in company 'aaa'
changeCompany('bbb')
{
// default company is now 'bbb'
custtable = NULL;
while select custtable
{
// Custtable is now selected in company 'aaa'
}
```

```
}

// default company is now set back to 'aaa' again
changeCompany('ccc')
{
// default company is now 'ccc'
custtable = NULL;
// clear Custtable to let the select work on the new
default company
while select custtable
{
// Custtable is now selected in company 'ccc'
}
}
// default company is now 'aaa' again
}
```

Question 124: Opening Form in Maximized mode

I have a form with the requirement that it should always open in Maximized mode by default.

Can you help me with this?

A: Yes, definitely. You need to add the following to your form's run() method:

```
#define.SC_MAXIMIZE (61488)
#define.WM_SYSCOMMAND (0x0112)
super();
WinAPI::SendMessage(element.hWnd(), #WM_SYSCOMMAND,
#SC_MAXIMIZE, '');
```

Question 125: Variable declaration X++ versus CLR?

I have noticed I can declare an X++ variable as follows:

```
str a , b, c;
```

Or

```
str a
str b
str c
```

Either one is fine, but when I try to declare a ClrObject:

```
ClrObject a, b, c;
```

I can't; it must be done like:

```
ClrObject a;
ClrObject b;
ClrObject c;
```

Is there a way to perform this similar to X++ types?

A: I think you must distinguish between objects and variables. You can also declare variables this way in C#:

```
String a, b, c;
```

Whereas you also must separate each object declaration on each line in C#:

```
Objecttype objecthandle;
Objecttype objecthandle;
```

Question 126: EP-Standard WEBGRID & its Header Label

```
WebForm: EPCustTableList
WebGrid: WebGridCust
Field: CustTable_Phone
```

How does this Object show the Label 'Telephone' in its header on the webpage?

Where are the properties for the CustTable Fields display header text applied and set?

I have searched through the Objects tree and investigated the Table itself, but I did not find any reference to 'Telephone'. The field name is 'Phone'.

How does it render 'Telephone' in the EP?

A: Short Answer:

The labels come from the extended datatypes.

Long Answer:

If you look at the EPCustTableList webform, you will see that there are 2 tables listed under the DataSources node (CustTable and SysTransactionSum).

The datasource custtable is a reference to a table in the AOT called custTable.

In the AOT, if you open the data dictionary, and then expand the Tables node, you can scroll down and find a table called custTable (as you have done).

If you expand the custTable and look at the fields, you will see there is a field called Phone. If you right click on this field and select properties, you will see that this field uses an extended datatype called Phone.

If you now close the table's node of the AOT, and open up the Extended Data Types node, you will see an entry for an extended data type called Phone. Right click it and select properties, and you will notice that the label says "Telephone".

It's a bit confusing, but also very powerful in that if you use extended datatypes properly; a change made to a label in the system will be reflected through the entire system.

Question 127: Getting sessionId or workspaceId

Is there an ID that I can get that will distinguish the current session from another?

I found the method in InfoLog.getWorkspaceList() which returns a container that looks like it has id's for the different workspaces.

Is there a way to tell which of these numbers refer to my current workspace?

A: The list contains a list of window handles. You can identify the current workspace window handle with infoLog.hWnd(1);

Below is a code example:

```
static void Job1(Args _args)
{
int idx;
int hWnd;
container con;
;

setPrefix("This workspace");
hWnd = conpeek(infoLog.getWorkspaceList(),1);
info(strFmt('HWND=%1 Text=%2', hWnd,
WinAPI::getWindowText(hWnd)));

idx = 1;
con = infoLog.getWorkspaceList();

setPrefix("All workspaces");

while (idx <= conlen(con))
{
hWnd = conpeek(con, idx);
info(strFmt('HWND=%1 Text=%2', hWnd,
WinAPI::getWindowText(hWnd)));
idx++;
}
}
```

Question 128: Read file from directory

My job requires me to constantly read from a directory. If there is a file, I have to move this file to another directory. The file also has to be modified or renamed before being moved.

How do I do this from AX?

A: Here's an example of how to rename a file:

```
client static void renameClientFile(str _fileName)
{
str newFileName;
str dir, fn, ext, newDir;
;
if (WinAPI::fileExists(_fileName))
{
[dir, fn, ext] = fileNameSplit(_fileName);
//newDir = ...
newFileName = strFmt("%1%2%3",
newDir,
fn,
ext);
WinAPI::moveFile(_fileName, newFileName);
}
}
```

You have to be careful if that file is located on server or client; most of the WinAPI file methods also have client counterparts.

Check the AsciiIO, BinaryIO classes in AOT/System documentation if you want to modify the file.

Question 129: Using DataAreaID as a Table Index

I have a table that has information stored for each company. My primary key should be DataAreaID.

Is it possible to use the DataAreaID as an 'Index' in AX?

When I try it, I get this SQL error:

```
"Cannot execute a data definition language command on
(). The SQL database has issued an error. Problems
during SQL data dictionary synchronization.
The operation failed. Synchronize failed on 1
table(s)"
```

A: Set the SaveDataPerCompany table-flag to 'false' if you prefer to "see" the records from every company.

Question 130: Filter Button

Has anyone created a 'Button' (called Filter) on a form which does exactly what the Ctrl+F3 does?

Can you tell me how this is done?

A: You can add a Command button and then set the Command property to 'Filter Records'.

Question 131: AX4 debugger missing values

Can you give a clue as to what MS has done to AX4 debugger since the object/variable values are missing in 'watch' and 'variables' windows?

Or is it something that I just overlooked?

A: The functions are still there. For some reason, the variable name column takes the whole screen. The values are hidden off the right side of your screen. Just drag the little slider over to make the values visible.

Question 132: Grid Label

I want to change the grid's field labels but I don't know how to do it.

Which method will I use to change labels?

I have one form CustInfo and one datasource table CustInformation and I use one grid [Grid:CustInf] and have 12 different fields from CustInformation. I want to change the labels' text on the grid fields for this form named 'custinfo'.

How can I change this by programming?

I changed the properties on 'AutoDeclaration' to yes. I don't want to use label fields on the properties though.

A: Since you've already set the autodeclaration to be yes, you can refer to the particular field in your code. Try something like this in the init method of the form:

```
void init()
{
super();
...
myField.label("My new label");
...
}
```

Question 133: FormTreeControl - FormTreeIt

I created a tree node in a FormTreeControl:

```
treeItemIdx = SysFormTreeControl::addTreeItem(
Tree,"Hello", rootidx, 'Data',imageRes, false);
```

I later changed the display text and used the following:

```
int idx = tree.getSelection();
FormTreeItem formTreeItem;
;
formTreeItem = tree.getItem(idx);
formTreeItem.text("there"); // change the node
display text (label)
element.redraw(); // refresh the tree visuals
```

Did I miss something? Is it possible to change the node display text in the tree once the node is created?

A: You can try this code instead:

```
tree.setItem(formTreeitem);
```

Question 134: Searching for specific EDTs

I'm new to AX. I am in the process of creating a new table. I wish to use existing EDTs for my fields.

I want to add a field of type: string & length > 60 or a Real field with length 15 & decimals 2.

How do you easily search for EDTs with specific criterion like type, length, etc from the host of EDTs available?

A: Try to right click the Extended Data Types node in the AOT and select 'Find'. In this dialog, there is a field called Search. Choose "All nodes". Having done this enables a fifth tab page called "Properties". Switch to this particular tab page.

Find e.g. the property called StringSize, tick the checkbox "Selected" and enter a value in the Range field. This is then evaluated using regular expressions and the match function.

You can also build your own extended data type list maker. Here is a small example job to get you started.

```
static void findEDT(Args _args)
{
UtilElements utilElements;
TreeNode edt;
int i = 0;
;
while select utilElements
where utilElements.recordType ==
UtilElementType::ExtendedType
{
edt = SysTreeNode::findNodeInLayer(
UtilElementType::ExtendedType,
utilElements.name, utilElements.parentId,
utilElements.utilLevel);

info(strFmt('Name: %1, Properties: %2, %3'
, utilElements.name
, edt.AOTgetProperties()
, edt.toString()
```

```
));
if ( i == 10 ) break; else i++; // just the first 10
}
}
```

There are some ID conversion functions available in the AOT;
from here it is a little bit of trial and error.

Question 135: infolog.viewUpdate, write to top in Axapta Programming

How can I make the infolog scroll to include the last line?

In a long running job, I wrote many lines to infolog. I call viewUpdate to refresh infolog so the end user can see data during the job. However the infolog does not scroll down and only the top xx lines are visible. The end user cannot scroll while the job is still running.

A: I suggest that you use the message window instead. This already has the functionality you seek.

The following job demonstrates how to use it:

```
static void MessageWinExample(Args _args)
{
MessageWin MessageWin;
InventTable inventTable;
;

// Activate messagewindow
MessageWin = infolog.messageWin();
MessageWin.activate();

startLengthyOperation();

// Some random long-running operation
while select inventTable
where inventTable.ItemType == ItemType::Service
{
// Add text to the auto-updating messagewindow
MessageWin.addLine(StrFmt("Item: %1
%2",inventTable.ItemId,inventTable.ItemName));
// Sleep for 500 ms to make operation run for a long
time
sleep(500);
}

endLengthyOperation();
}
```

Question 136: Deactivate auto-complete

Is it possible to deactivate the auto-complete function on control level?

I need this not through the user options but just for a specific control.

A: You can use delAutoCompleteString:

```
public boolean modified()
{
boolean ret;
;

ret = super();

element.delAutoCompleteString(this);

return ret;
}
```

Question 137: Be interactive with a form or dialog through X++ code

Job A shows a form and waits for user interaction. However, I want to capture the form, do some operations like entering some values and close it at the end in another job through X++ code to simulate the manual interaction on the form.

Is this possible in Dynamics AX 4.0?

A: Yes, it is possible. You instantiate the form and you don't call 'form.wait' but instead continue to work with the form. When you're done then call form.closeOk().

Here is a sample:

```
FormRun form = null;
FormStringControl stringCtrl = null;
FormDateControl dateCtrl = null;
FormTabControl tabCtrl = null;
Args formParams = new Args();
;
// STEP 1: Instantiate and display the form
formParams.name('Introduction');
form = classFactory.formRunClass(formParams);
form.init();
form.run();

// STEP 2: Get control objects and set some values
stringCtrl = form.design().controlName('StringEdit');
dateCtrl = form.design().controlName('DateEdit');
tabCtrl = form.design().controlName('Tab');

stringCtrl.text('Homer Simpson');
dateCtrl.dateValue(04\03\2005);

// STEP 3: Validations
if (stringCtrl.text() == 'Homer Simpson')
{
print 'Control ' + stringCtrl.name() + ' validation
has failed!';
print 'Current value: ' + stringCtrl.text();
}
```

```
if (dateCtrl.dateValue() == 04\03\2005)
{
print 'Control ' + dateCtrl.name() + ' validation has
failed!';
print 'Current value: ' +
date2str(dateCtrl.dateValue(), -1, -1, -1, -1, -1,
-1);
}
// STEP 4: Close the form (and save changes)
form.closeOk();
```

Question 138: Delete all data in a temporary table

What is the best way to delete all the data stored in a temporary table?

I was looping over the table and deleting each record one by one like this:

```
====================
while select myTempTable
{
myTempTable.delete();
}
====================
```

Is there a better way of doing this?

A: Yes, there is. You can use delete_from. For example:

```
delete_from myTempTable
```

Question 139: Programmable Section

Can one incorporate a programmable section in the footer of an Axapta report?

A: Yes, you can. Just override the 'ExecuteSection' method of the footer. In there, do an element.execute(..) to run your programmable section.

Question 140: Select a record based on TableID and RecID

If I have a record ID and a table ID, how can I go about selecting that record into a common buffer and access its fields?

For example, SalesTable has AddressRefRecID and AddressRefTableID.

Initially I was going to do something like this but I know there must be a better way:

```
===========================================
if(AddressRefTableID == tablenum(Address))
{
select address where address.recid = AddressRefRecID
}
else if(AddressRefTableID == tablenum(CustTable))
{
select custtable where custtable.recid ==
AddressRefRecID
}
===========================================
```

Can you give any suggestions?

A: You can use the following instead:

```
//select record using common and dictTable
Common getRecord(tableId _tableId, RecId _recId)
{
Common common;
DictTable dictTable;
;

dictTable = new DictTable(_tableId);
common = dictTable.makeRecord();
select firstOnly common where common.RecId == _recId;

return common;
}

//access fields in common buffer
void showFieldInfoDemo()
```

```
{
Common common;
;

common = this.getRecord(tableNum(CustTrans),
4086575);

info(common.(fieldNum(CustTrans, AccountNum)));
}
```

Question 141: Clicking on grid makes form to appear

I want get form B to appear when form A grip > text clicked.

Where should I create the method?

1. in the datasource?
2. Design > textfield?
3. or both?

As I go through, there is no method On_Clicked(). I tried to create a method manually by creating this:

```
on_clicked()
{
return B_table;
}
```

I don't know if this syntax is correct as I am new in Axapta.

A: You just need to override one of these methods: MouseDbClick, MouseDown, MouseUp.

Question 142: NET Enums in X++

I'm trying to learn more with AX4.0. I'm trying to use .NET classes within X++ by adding a reference to a .NET assembly, for example System.Data.dll. There are instances where I need to pass an enum value to a method parameter, but I can't find a way to declare and use a .NET enum type (for example, System.Data.DbType) variable.

Do you know of a way to declare and use .NET enum types in X++?

A: You can declare the variable as a normal in X++ and use ClrInterop::parseClrEnum to get the specific values as in the following sample.

```
static void EnumSample(Args _args)
{
int i;
;

i =
ClrInterop::parseClrEnum("System.IO.FileAccess","Read
");
print i;
pause;
}
```

Question 143: Update data source

I want to update the form 'MarkupTrans' when I modify 'TaxGroup' in the Sales Table form. Since MarkupTrans is not added as a data source in Sales Table form, I am finding it difficult to update the MarkupTrans data source and the form.

Can you tell me what needs to be done?

A: If the active method is called on the Sales Table data source, the linkActive method will be called on any forms that have been opened from the Sales Table form. In other words, you only have to call the active method on the data source when the tax group is modified or when the record is saved.

Question 144: Best way to get a table ID

What is the best way to get a table ID?

I tried this:

```
CustTable c;
...
c.tableID;
```

Is there a better way of getting that value so that I don't need to declare a CustTable cursor?

A: You can use the tableNum function. For example:

```
tableNum(CustTable);
```

Question 145: Duplex Printing

Can you give me pointers on how to print on both sides of reports from AX?

I need it to be driven from the class running the report, so the users don't have to set it up each and every time.

A: Try using this display method:

```
display str setEscCodeDuplex()
{
element.setEscapeSequence(num2char(27)+'&l1S');
return element.passThrough(num2Char(27)+'&l1S');
}
```

Then make a string-field in your report header which calls this method.

Note: This only works if your printer supports escape-codes.

Question 146: Display method name or path on an error message in exception handle

Do you know how I can display the name and possibly the path of a method dynamically when I handle exceptions?

For example, I have a new method myNewMethod() on the SalesFormLetter class. I have some code in this method that I have surrounded with a try catch block and I want the catch to throw the name and possibly the path of the method I am in.

```
void myNewMethod() {
try {
//do something
} catch (exception::error) {
//this is where I want to dynamically display the
name of the
method. So something like:
throw error("SalesFormLetter\myNewMethod()");
}
}
```

A: Try the following instead:

The name of the class:

```
classId2Name(classIdGet(this));
```

The name of the class and the method:

```
funcname();
```

The callstack:

```
int i;
str callStack;
container con;
;

con = xSession::xppCallStack();

for (i = 1; i <= conlen(con); i += 2)
{
```

```
if (callStack != "")
{
callStack += " ";
}

callStack += strfmt("%1(%2)", conpeek(con, i),
conpeek(con, i + 1));
}
```

Question 147: Prevent deletion of Invoiced Sales Orders

How can I prevent the deletion of invoiced Sales Orders and Purchase Orders?

A: You can prevent the deletion of Invoiced Sales Orders by modifying salestabletype.validatedelete().

Question 148: Strange error in changing BOMConsistOf form

I am using Ax3.0 SP5 KR1. I was having some strange problem on changing the BOMConsistOf form. After I change the form, an error showing "The Table does not contain this field." in BOMConsistOf.init() method which is referring to ItemTypeIcon.imageList(imageList.imageList()); line. Axapta error shows that the ItemTypeIcon can not be found in the table.

I searched through the whole application, but I can't find any object named with ItemTypeIcon.

Do you know what the problem may be and how can I overcome this problem if I change the form?

A: The ItemTypeIcon is an autoDeclared variable for the WindowControl in the grid (GridBOM). You may have accidentally deleted that control or renamed it.

Question 149: Dynamic access to titlefield1

I am modifying the InventTable form, changing the form caption, overview ItemId label, etc. The title data source is set to InventTable, and the table's titlefield1 and 2 are set to ItemId and ItemName.

Even though I can change the form caption and control labels, I haven't found a way to dynamically change the title fields of a title data source. I could change it statically, but this is not an option.

Can you give any ideas in changing the title fields in code?

A: Whenever you can use the standard caption, which is created by the kernel in the way you described, it is a great feature. But it can be really annoying to set it manually.

You cannot change the title fields of the table at runtime. The way it is done in form SalesTable might help: no TitleDatasource is set, but they set up the title in method setCaptionText(), which is called in linkActive() and active().

Another alternative you can consider is overwriting the caption method on InventTable (on table level). This way you can build the whole caption yourself.

To be sure, that you don't do this in the wrong places, you could check that the buffer is used in an InventTable form. An example of which is the following:

```
public str caption()
{
str ret;

if (this.isFormDataSource() &&
this.dataSource().formRun().name() ==
formstr(InventTable))
{
```

```
ret = strfmt("Dynamically build caption %1 ...",
this.ItemId, ...);
}
else
{
ret = super();
}

return ret;
}
```

Question 150: Edit info text on top of EPSalesTableCreate

In the enterprise portal (en-us) you can select in the menu 'quick entry'. This opens the EPSalesTableCreate webform. On top of this form you will see a title 'Quick Entry'. Underneath you get some text that says: 'You can use this form to quickly add items to your shopping cart by using the entry line at the bottom. Use the + icon...'

I'm now trying to find the label, table, resource that holds this text. It will help a lot to know where this text is triggered.

When you browse the portal in Dutch (nl-be) or French (fr-be) those lines are not displayed.

Do have any idea as to how this could be done?

A: It is stored in the help text of the tree nodes.

```
\Menu Items\Action\EPSalesTableCreate
\Menu Items\Action\EPSalesTableCreateCSS
```

Just add them in the AOT and edit them by selecting one and then press F1.

Question 151: Inner select

Can I do an inner select in Axapta?

Something like:

```
select instance
where instance.field in (select field from instance2
where
instance2.field2 == value);
```

A: Yes, you definitely can. Quoting from the Axapta Developer's Guide:

Inner join: selects records from the main table that have matching records in the joined table - and vice versa. In other words, you get one record for each match and records without related records are eliminated from the result.

```
static void Job37(Args _args)
{
CustTable custTable;
CustTrans custTrans;
AccountNum accountNum;
;

accountNum = "100000"; //set a valid account number
here.

while select custTable
join AmountMST from custTrans
where custTable.AccountNum == custTrans.AccountNum &&
custTable.AccountNum == accountNum
{
info(strfmt("%1", custTrans.AmountMST));
}
}
```

Question 152: Grid DataMethod

I have a data source and I want to add one (1) independent column to the grid. This column will be of the type checkbox so I can check some rows and afterwards process the checked rows.

How can I add such an independent row?

I already know that I need to create a datamethod in the datasource, but my fields stay empty, even after I checked a box.

My code of the method:

```
---------------------------------------------------

edit str dummyValue(boolean _set,
FCS_FMC_RuleArgument _ruleArgument,
str _value)
{
;
if (_set)
{
this.refresh();
}
else
{
return grdArguments.
return spec.findRefId(_ruleArgument.TableId,
_ruleArgument.RecId).0seValue;
}

return _value;
}

---------------------------------------------------
```

A: Your problem seems to be that you don't store the arguments to the edit method anywhere, so Axapta has no way of knowing which records you have selected. There's two ways to resolve this:

1. Make a new NoYesId field on your table, and store the value there, or
2. Use a map (map(types::Integer,types::Record)).

The first solution requires you to change your data model (i.e adding a field to a table) and gives you an extra overhead (although very small) for the Data base Server, and also requires you to control which user has made the mark. The second can be handled purely in X++ code and will hence only affect the client, and no concurrency control is required.

To see an example of how to use maps to control which records have been marked in a grid, look at \Forms\ReqTransPo. The first checkbox "MarkOverview" on the grid "GridReqPo" is such a field.

Question 153: Lexical Error

I have a macro with static strings in it. When I add the following two lines, my classes do not compile anymore.

```
#define.bracketOpen ('(')
#define.bracketClose (')')
```

Can you give any clues as to how to deal with this?

A: That is the first time I saw a solution where a label is used in a Macro. Anyway, you can try this:

```
static void parenthesisJob(Args _args)
{
#define.rightParenthesis(41)
#define.leftParenthesis(40)
;
info(strFmt('%1 sssSSHht... %2',
num2char(#leftParenthesis),
num2char(#rightParenthesis) ));
}
```

Question 154: About Axapta reports

I want to know information about Axapta reports; like who run the reports (empl, time, day), how many times, etc.

Is there any way to get this kind of information from Axapta?

A: There is no way in standard Axapta to get that information. You will have to make a modification. The 'SysReportRun' can be a starting point.

Question 155: Importing Labels

What is the best way to import labels if you are using the .aod file?

When importing an XPO file, there is an option to import labels. But if you use the .aod file to ship a complete application layer, how can I import labels?

A: If you deploy an AOD file, you should simply distribute the label files (axXXX-YY.ald) too, so your "application package" consists of the AOD files and all the needed label files.

Question 156: To access application directory runtime

Is there any method to access application directory runtime?

I need to read the label source files, etc via COM-connector.

A: Yes, there is. You need to use:

```
info(xInfo::directory(DirectoryType::Appl));
```

Question 157: Problems updating a ProjJournalTable record

In X++ code, I have the following:

```
// Now update the Journal Table Entry
JournalID = ProjJournalTable.JournalId;
//ProjJournalTable updProjJournal;
updProjJournal = ProjJournalTable::Find(JournalID,
true);
updProjJournal.NumOfLines = LineNum;
updProjJournal.ProjQty = TotalHours;
updProjJournal.update();
```

I get this error when the update runs:

```
"Can't update record because it is not selected for
update".
```

When I debug this section of code, the recid and forupdate appears in the watch window on updProjJournal and it seems to call update correctly.

Can you give an idea on why I am getting this error?

A: You have not encapsulated your update function inside a transaction scope.

Change your code to this:

```
// Now update the Journal Table Entry
JournalID = ProjJournalTable.JournalId;
//ProjJournalTable updProjJournal;
ttsbegin; <--------
updProjJournal = ProjJournalTable::Find(JournalID,
true);
updProjJournal.NumOfLines = LineNum;
updProjJournal.ProjQty = TotalHours;
updProjJournal.update();
ttscommit; <---------
```

Question 158: Accessing Checkboxes

I have added to the ProdParmRelease form four check boxes on the General Tab. What I would like to do is when the OK button is clicked, check each of these check boxes to see if they are checked, and if so perform a piece of code.

The problem is when I override the clicked method on the OK button; I do not know how to access these checkboxes.

Can you show to me how this is done?

A: Set the Autodeclaration option on each check box to yes. After that you could access the checkboxes from the whole form. Think about writing one method that does the validation and call that method from the click() method or probably the closeOk() from that form.

Question 159: Save a file with the help of a SaveDialog

I want to save a file with the help of a SaveDialog. In my form is a button called "Save to file". If the user presses this button, a save dialog should appear. The user chooses the path and click "Save". At this time the file should be saved to the chosen path.

I've already read and understood the tutorial, named "tutorial_Form_file". But in this example the "Save button" is combined with a "StringEdit". I want to open the dialog by pressing a button, created by myself.

Do you have an idea how I could do this?

A: You can open save file dialog by using Dialog and DialogField Classes. Put the following code to 'clicked event' of the button.

```
void clicked()
{
Dialog dlg = New dialog("Save file");
DialogField df = dlg.addField(typeId(FileNameSave));
;

if (dlg.run())
{
box::info(Global::fileNameTrim(df.value()));
}
}
```

Question 160: ListIterator problem in 3T

I encountered this problem when using LisIterator in 3T.

I wrote these in form: InventTransRegister

```
* * * * * * * * * * * * * * * *
Object m_object;
List m_list;
ListIterator m_li;
;
m_object=element.args().caller();
m_list=m_object.parmList(); //get a list from caller,
correct

m_li=new ListIterator(m_list); //m_li==null
while(m_li.more()) //report error here
{
......;
m_li.next();
}
```

In 2T, this works perfectly, but in 3T, it reports error "Object not initialized". I debug it; find that correct list is given to variable m_list in this code:

```
m_list=m_object.parmList();
```

but the next sentence:
```
m_li=new ListIterator(m_list);
```

```
makes m_li=null
```

Then the error occured.

How do I fix this?

A: Here is a clue:

<In 2T, this works perfectly, but in 3T, it reports error "Object not initialized".>

The iterator must be on the same CS side as List it traverses. Make sure you create both List and ListIterator in classes which are both declared like 'RunOn=Server' or 'RunOn=Client'.

See AX help for more details: kerndoc://classes/listIterator

Question 161: End of file

I would like to open a file and delete the last character of that file.

How can I do that easily?

A: Here is an example:

```
TextBuffer textBuffer = new TextBuffer();
FileName fileName = "c:\\test.txt";
;

textBuffer.fromFile(fileName);
textBuffer.setText(textBuffer.subStr(1,
strLen(textBuffer.getText())-1 ));
textBuffer.toFile(fileName);
```

Question 162: EDT Crash

Have you encountered an EDT crash?

The Standard EDT InventQty is supposed to be real. However, I do not know how it become a String EDT which was under the VAR layer. I was not able to revert back the InventQty EDT back to real. I even tried to view its properties, but my program will restart automatically.

How do I solve this problem?

A: An option is to run a job like this in the VAR layer.

```
static void Job1(Args _args)
{
treenode treenode;
;
treeNode = TreeNode::findNode("Data
Dictionary\\Extended Data
Types\\InventQty");
treeNode.AOTdelete();
}
```

Question 163: To retrieve the field(s) range on a form

In my form, I want to see the criteria that a user has selected/filtered.

I need to get the records which are displayed in the dialog filter after the user has made a selection on the form.

Is this possible?

A: Yes, it is. You need to use:

```
<YourTable>_ds.queryRun().query().dataSourceName(<You
rDataSourceName>).range.value
```

Question 164: Users Online

Can you tell me why the information in the Users Online Active Sessions is different from each work station?

If I log on to the 3 tier thin from my work station, the type in the users online active sessions window display 'Thin'. If I walk over to another users work station it may display NotAos or from another user's station it may display it correctly as Thin.

A: I guess that you are using multiple AOSs in a cluster.

Clients will see other clients on the same AOS as Thin, but those sessions connected to a different AOS will display as NotAOS.

Question 165: Getting meta-information for menu items

For retrieving meta-information from tables and field, you can use the classes Dictionary, DictTables and DictFields. I'm looking for a way to do the same with menus and menu items.

What I am trying to do is get a list of all the available menu items including their references to parent menus. The properties I'm interested in are the menu item IDs, menu item names and menu item labels.

Can you help me?

A: Yes, I can. The sample code below may help you:

```
TreeNode t;
Counter c;
void traverseMenuFunctions(MenuItemType mft)
{
treeNodeIterator it;
TreeNode menuItemsNode;
switch(mft)
{
case MenuItemType::Action:
menuItemsNode = TreeNode::findNode('\\Menu
Items\\Action');
break;
case MenuItemType::Display:
menuItemsNode = TreeNode::findNode('\\Menu
Items\\Display');
break;
case MenuItemType::Output:
menuItemsNode = TreeNode::findNode('\\Menu
Items\\Output');
break;
}
it = menuItemsNode.AOTiterator();
t = it.next();
while(t)
{
print (t.AOTname());
t = it.next();
c++;
```

```
}
}
c = 0;
traverseMenuFunctions(MenuItemType::Action);
traverseMenuFunctions(MenuItemType::Display);
traverseMenuFunctions(MenuItemType::Output);
print 'Total is ' + int2str(c);
pause;
```

Then class MenuItem, MenuFunction may be helpful to get the information you like as well.

Question 166: Get the application/environment from X++

Is there a way to get the name of the current environment/application (i.e. in our case PROD or DEV) that you are in using X++?

A: Yes, there is. You need to print xinfo::configuration();.

Question 167: Changes in tables

If I add one or more fields to a table, it sometimes takes minutes to see these fields on a forms data source.

Can you tell me what I have to do to make the update of a form data source faster?

A: Try to right click the form and select "Restore".

Question 168: parameter character of num2str function

I don't understand the purpose of the character parameter of the num2str function. I already read the documentation, but I don't understand how this parameter works.

What is the use of parameter?

A: It determines the minimum length of the string created by the function. For example, if you use num2str (1234,12,2,1,2) you will get 1,234.00 padded out to a string 12 characters long.

If on the other hand you use num2str (1234,1,2,1,2), then the result will have no leading spaces.

The results of the 2 expressions are 1,234.00 (with leading spaces) and 1,234.00.

Question 169: Multi-table Quotation report

I have a report which is based on the table CustQuotationJour for the SalesQuotation report; it came preinstalled. I would like to add two fields from the SalesTable table, DeliveryName and DeliveryAddress.

These are the steps I took:

1. Dragged SalesTable into SalesQuotation - Data Sources - Query - Data Sources - CustQuotationJour - Data Sources. A relationship was created:

CustQuotationJour.SalesId == SalesTable.SalesId

2. Added the fields SalesTable.DeliveryName and SalesTable.DeliveryAddress into PageHeader:Quotation.

3. Saved and compiled the Generated Design.

When I ran the report, the new fields were not displayed or they did not display any data; I'm not sure which. I ran a query in SQL Server and found the data, so I know it exists in SalesTable:

```
SELECT s.DeliveryName, s.DeliveryAddress
FROM SalesTable s
INNER JOIN CustQuotationJour c ON c.SalesId =
s.SalesId
WHERE c.QuotationnDocNum = 'xxxx'
```

I'm not sure if I should add or reconfigure any objects.

Can you give any suggestion on how to proceed from here?

A: DeliveryName and DeliveryAddress are already in CustConfirmJour. You can use these fields.

You can add some display methods on the quotation header, so you don't need the datasource. For example:

```
display Addressing deliveryAddress()
```

```
{
return
SalesTable::find(custQuotationJour.SalesId).DeliveryA
ddress;
}
```

And generate a control on the report which uses the display method.

Question 170: Web portal problems

I have this problem with a portal in Axapta 3.0. If the logon screen has been waiting a long time (half an hour or so), and then you log on, the portal enters an empty page. It's not completely empty; it contains a header, and the welcome message. However, no menus exist, and no buttons or links.

Why is this happening?

A: This problem depends on the session time out when you create your web site. The default time is 20 minutes but you can expand it to 1 hour if you like.

Index

3 tier.............................93, 177
ABC Codes..........................13
accents..............................39
access. .8, 20, 40, 46, 70, 74, 78, 97, 102, 152, 168, 170
Accessing Checkboxes....170
accumulated amount........83
ACP (Ansi Code Page).....121
Active Directory Import...43
Active Directory import wizard............................23
active method.................156
active user.........................93
active().............................161
actively clean up..............40
ActiveX control.................59
ActiveX Error...................59
actual button...................107
AD Import.........................43
AD structure.....................45
add-ons.............................40
ADO.................................108
AIF..............................36, 37
Aisle-Rack-Shelf sequence 23
Allocation..........................80
Alt+W+A...........................42
aoc-files.............................55
AOS connection management.................93
AOS licenses......................58
AOT.......34, 70, 77, 124, 137, 138, 140, 145, 146, 163
application directory runtime........................168
Application pool...............33
application/environment 180
arguments........109, 129, 165
arguments list.................109
Authentication problems. 46

automatic journal postings 12
Automatic Processing.......65
automatic report..............12
automatic route consumption.................89
AX.....1, 2, 8, 9, 11, 12, 15, 18, 22, 23, 24, 25, 26, 30, 33, 35, 38, 43, 46, 47, 48, 49, 50, 51, 55, 59, 60, 61, 64, 65, 66, 70, 71, 72, 76, 102, 114, 121, 129, 140, 141, 145, 149, 157, 173
AX Team Server Setup Installation Error..........61
AX4 debugger.................142
Axapta...8, 10, 15, 19, 20, 22, 24, 28, 31, 35, 36, 39, 42, 44, 46, 48, 51, 52, 53, 54, 55, 57, 58, 62, 63, 73, 75, 78, 80, 81, 84, 85, 87, 89, 90, 91, 92, 93, 94, 95, 98, 99, 100, 101, 102, 103, 104, 107, 114, 122, 147, 151, 154, 160, 164, 165, 167, 184
Axapta Batch Server Installation....................63
Axapta HR.......................44
Axapta Localization.101, 102
Axapta Object Cache files. 55
Axapta Object Server 4.0. .15
Axapta Purchase Orders...99
Axapta report.................151
Axapta v3 AOS environment 53
backup..................29, 45, 83
BaseEnum.................115, 116
Batch journals................124
batch process..................65
batch server..............63, 124
BatchJob.........................22

BatchQue............................22
BatchRuns..........................22
Best Practice Checks........40
best practice errors...........40
best practice violations....40
best practices...................28
BOM line data..................34
BOM lines.........................34
BOMConsistOf form........160
BOMs...........................34, 50
bomtreeDesigner.............126
Boolean value..................112
Brazilian localization......102
breakpoint.........67, 125, 129
bridge account................103
browsing............................93
bump.................................82
Business Connector...19, 30,
  32, 33, 47
Business Connector Proxy
  account...........................33
Button Hotkeys...............107
caching..............................73
Call debugger..................125
calling code.....................112
capacity calculations.........75
Capacity load....................89
capacity reservation.........89
capture............................149
catch block......................158
change company statement
 133
Changing EDT Type.........111
Changing the language in
  Axapta 4.0.....................24
child reference................128
class.9, 11, 19, 20, 33, 52, 63,
  105, 109, 112, 114, 117,
  118, 121, 129, 157, 158, 179
class code (methods).......114
clicked event...................171
Clicking on grid..............154
client folder......................83
client tracing checkbox.....35

client-authentication........58
Close All Open Forms.......42
CLOSE mark....................128
CLR..................................136
cluster.............................177
code cleanups....................60
Code Migration...............114
code routine....................118
code upgrade.....................60
codepage.........................121
Collection class Map........117
color code........................108
COM object...........11, 19, 20
COM-connector...............168
Combination cost price....88
Command button............142
commented lines.............116
common buffer................152
common standard cost price
 88
compare function.............66
compatible.........................98
Compilation Errors.........100
complete application layer
 168
concurrency control........166
concurrent users..............64
configured.........................47
Consistency Checks..........28
console........................36, 65
console application...........36
consumed goods..............72
control9, 11, 74, 89, 115, 128,
  148, 149, 160, 161, 166,
  183
control level...................148
controls....................59, 110
correspondence class list 114
Ctrl+F3...........................142
currency code...................71
Currency Converter...........71
current costs.....................85
current workspace..........139
customization...................72

customized value..............13
custTable.................137, 164
CustTable cursor.............156
Damgaard Data A/S as
    Axapta...........................8
data conversion................13
data dictionary...27, 35, 137,
    141
Data Dictionary.........73, 175
data maintenance.............28
data model......................166
data source name..............18
data structure..................28
data transfer.....................56
DataAreaId......................120
DataAreaID.....................141
database engine................53
Database Log Cleanup......28
Database Server size.........97
Database transfer..............45
DataSource......................113
datasource custtable.......137
Deactivate auto-complete
   148
Dedicated link..................56
default language...............24
default language codes.....24
default time.....................184
default web service..........36
Deferred Tax...................103
delAutoCompleteString..148
delayed service restart......17
Delete.24, 41, 42, 63, 69, 70,
    74, 89, 151, 174
Delete bom records..........24
delta................................60
deploy.......................30, 168
Deploying webparts..........30
depreciation.....................76
depreciation run...............76
dialog...25, 145, 149, 171, 176
dialog filter.....................176
display method. .77, 157, 183
display-only.....................74

DMO Company................32
document handling..........97
domain user account........20
dotNet -Connector...........22
drag-over nodes..............126
drop method...................126
Duplex Printing...............157
Duplicate qualifications...44
Dynamic access...............161
Dynamic Grid Label........110
dynamically......110, 158, 161
Edit info text...................163
edit method..............40, 165
EDT crash.......................175
End of file.......................174
Ended Production orders. 63
enterprise portal. .19, 32, 33,
    38, 46, 58, 97, 163
enterprise portal customer
    role..............................58
Enterprise Portal Error
    message..........................19
Enterprise Portal Site.......38
entire inventory...............50
enum value.....................155
EP..................33, 46, 47, 137
EP-Standard WEBGRID.137
EPSalesTableCreate........163
ERPs................................64
Error Account..................84
error log file....................20
escape-codes...................157
event log..........................78
event viewer.....................78
Excel COM Export
    Performance...............122
exception handle.............158
exceptions.......................158
Extended Data Types node
    ....138, 145
extended datatypes. 137, 138
extension.........................55
external application..........39
external website..............105

extra overhead..................166
fast pick items...................13
Faster export..................108
field(s) range..................176
filter..........................42, 115
Filter Button..................142
final tax account..............103
Financial Statement...83, 84
find criterion....................42
finished feature.................12
finite capacity scheduling.82
Firm................................80
first costing.....................85
first NIC..........................56
first sales tax code...........103
Fixed Asset Journal..........76
flat XML file....................108
footer.............................151
Forecast Consumption.....54
form....13, 26, 27, 33, 34, 40,
  41, 42, 44, 50, 65, 69, 70,
  79, 81, 87, 88, 109, 115,
  116, 118, 127, 131, 135,
  142, 143, 149, 150, 154,
  156, 160, 161, 163, 170,
  171, 172, 176, 180
form caption....................161
FormTreeControl....126, 144
FormTreeIt.....................144
free connections...............93
free text..........................119
Free Text Invoice..............76
full trust..........................61
functionality..26, 44, 67, 92,
  147
Gantt chart.......................59
Generated Design...........182
get a table ID..................156
Getting sessionId...........139
Grid DataMethod............165
Grid Label..................110, 143
Hard................................80
Header Label..................137
help text..........................163

higher build......................92
Highest version................98
host................................145
IE settings.......................47
if 39
IIS.........................32, 33, 47
import screen..................129
importing 23, 34, 73, 97, 168
Importing BOMs...............34
Importing Labels............168
importing users................23
Importing XPO Error.....129
inbound docks..................67
independent column.......165
individual cells...............108
individual standard cost
  price............................88
infolog scroll..................147
infolog.viewUpdate.........147
init method......109, 120, 143
inner select....................164
instantiate................22, 149
integrated windows
  authentication..............46
interactive......................149
Inventory. .13, 50, 67, 75, 79,
  80, 81, 86, 98, 112
inventory closing..............86
Inventory Closing............50
inventory dimension........80
Inventory dimension
  Location.......................67
Inventory lead time..........75
Inventory models groups. 79
Inventory parameters.......79
InventSumDelta..............112
InventSumDelta table.....112
InventTable77, 106, 113, 131,
  147, 161
InventTransRegister.......172
item master......................72
iterator..........................173

job. .51, 77, 82, 105, 106, 119, 120, 124, 133, 140, 145, 147, 149, 175
job times............................51
join.................41, 91, 112, 164
join order............................91
Kanji..............................102
Kerberos............................47
Kernel Rollup. 31, 35, 53, 57, 92
key combination................42
keyboard shortcut.............42
KR1..........35, 57, 83, 92, 160
KR2........................35, 53, 57
KR2/KR3 Installation......35
LAN IP..............................56
last line............................147
leading spaces.................181
Lexical Error....................167
linkActive method...........156
linkActive().......................161
ListIterator problem.......172
live......................................28
local administrator account 20
local drive...........................61
locations......................23, 67
locking............................112
locks.................................69
log disk.............................29
Logging.............................57
logon alias........................33
long running queries........29
lookup form.....................109
loop through...................115
macro...............................167
mail orders........................58
Maintenance Strategy......28
manual interaction.........149
manual record.................34
map...........117, 130, 165, 166
margin..............................13
Marking.....................80, 81
MarkupTrans.................156

master planning.........54, 81
master scheduling.............81
Maximized mode............135
MDAX 4.0..........................11
Memo type EDT..............119
message header.................37
meta-information............178
method.....25, 52, 63, 67, 77, 109, 112, 115, 118, 120, 126, 129, 131, 132, 139, 143, 154, 155, 156, 157, 158, 160, 161, 165, 168, 170
Microsoft Axapta Business Connector......................20
mid market segment companies....................64
Migration...........................60
minimum length..............181
Missing labels..................118
missing values.................142
mixed access....................94
MorphX.......................8, 133
MRP date...........................75
MSSQL database..............94
Multi-channel order processing.....................58
Multi-table Quotation report............................182
multiple attendees............26
Named Pipes protocol.......31
naming conventions.........55
native mode......................92
natively.............................60
NAV...................................64
NET Enums in X++........155
net off...............................54
network folder..................97
network names.................43
new payment proposal......41
new static data.................28
NIC/IP..............................56
non clustered AOS............73
normal......................8, 155

NTLM authentication.......47
num2str function.............181
number sequence.............69
objects. 8, 118, 122, 136, 149, 182
Objects tree......................137
ODBC connection.............94
on hand record.................81
on hand report.................98
operations scheduling......82
optimal query...................91
Optimistic Concurrency Checking........................57
OR ing in addRange().....132
outbound docks.................67
Output data......................133
Overlap quantity...............49
Overlap time.....................49
override.....131, 151, 154, 170
overwriting......................161
P&L and Balance Sheet....76
packing slip updating.......79
parameter character........181
part........8, 36, 37, 57, 79, 82
Partial costing..................85
partnersource.....21, 36, 102, 103
Passing multiple parameters 109
PDF Functionality............57
Pegging............................81
Performance Analysis......28
periodic form....................79
physical sales tax..............79
physically updated............99
picked...................80, 128
picking lines....................128
picking list journal..........50
picking route...................128
ping.................................56
port..................................78
Posting Profile.................76
Posting VAT.....................79
pre-filled.........................43

pre-populated text...........42
preconfigured master.aoc.55
preinstalled.....................182
Prevent deletion..............160
primary key.............131, 141
primary key violation......131
Production costing......50, 51
production environment..48
production journal...........69
production order..12, 49, 50, 51, 63, 82, 85
production parameters....89
Programmable Section....151
progressively update........89
Project and type Fixed-Price 68
Project Contract Item Consumption Pricing....72
ProjJournalTable record 169
proxy account.................47
query class......................95
Rapid Configuration Toolkit 21
Re-indexing....................28
re-scheduling.................82
Read file........................140
Realized consumption......51
Realized cost.................51
recalculation...................86
Recalculation...................50
RecID............................152
reconfigure....................182
reference lot...................81
reinstall.........................30
relate..............................14
reloading time.................29
Remote Procedure Call engine.........................25
Rename AOS instance......30
renamed...........30, 140, 160
report design...............120
report header.................157
reporting functionality.....92
reporting server..............18

Reporting Server Role......18
reserving stock.................112
Restore............................180
restriction.........................74
revenue........................13, 68
revenue scale.....................13
reverse registration..........99
reversing...........................99
Route for costing...............75
route operation..................12
routing card......................89
run time text file...............52
run() method.............115, 135
runtime......................94, 161
SaveDialog.......................171
Securing data.....................74
security issue...................100
serial/batch control..........80
server configuration utility
....35
session time.....................184
Shared application tree....73
Sharepoint site..................30
shortcut keys...................107
simulate...........................149
single operation..........12, 82
single reporting server......18
single test server AXTST...15
site templates....................46
skill-mapping....................44
Soft....................................80
source database.................18
SP1 User session no longer
valid..............................25
SP4 DIS layer...................103
specific EDTs...................145
spectrans...........................41
SQL 2005 Enterprise Client
....53
SQL Protocol 's'.................31
SQL Server Tracing Utilities
....57
SQL trace...........................29
Stability............................57

Stack trace............32, 36, 77
standard behavior.............44
standard caption..............161
standard code....................60
standard cost method.......85
Standard cost price..........88
standard filter..................115
standard function
strReplace.....................39
standard maintenance
strategy.........................28
start....17, 31, 40, 43, 46, 49,
50, 58, 61, 78, 82, 122, 127
start date...........................82
static strings....................167
statically..........................161
stock postings...................99
stored..........97, 141, 151, 163
String EDT.......................175
string expression.............133
string-field......................157
strings...............................39
Sub-contract.....................12
sub-contracting processes 12
sub-productions..............82
Supplementary items......118
Sync error..........................35
Synchronization...............28
Synchronizing Data-
Dictionary-ERROR.......27
syntax..............106, 133, 154
SysReportRun.................167
SysStartupCMD..............127
system tables....................111
table collection function. 124
Table Index......................141
table permissions issue....59
table-flag.........................141
TableID............................152
tableNum function..........156
tax group.........................156
TCP/IP..............................31
Team site...........................46
temporary table..95, 118, 151

test system.........................83
TextIO <> AsciiIO...........121
Thin..................................177
third-party........................72
Three (3) tier client..........63
three (3)-tier environment
....78
total capacity.....................97
transaction scope.............169
Transfer Orders.................67
transfer warehouse...........67
tree node...........................144
TreeNode class.................118
triggered...........................163
Trust-Worthy Computing 40
Try wait() method...........127
Unicode format.................121
uninstall.............................30
update..12, 13, 42, 50, 51, 57,
    79, 85, 89, 106, 113, 156,
    169, 180
Update data source.........156
update production costing
....85
updating....12, 51, 57, 79, 93,
    147, 169
upgrade documentation...48
upgraded exe.....................83
Upgrading to AX4.............92
URL encryption.................33
Usage of OLD folder.........66
User Admin........................14
user interaction...............149
Users Online.....................177
validation check...............70
validation rule...................44
value field.........................113
Value Model.......................76
VAR layer..........................175
Variable declaration X++
....136
variable declarations.......129
variables...................136, 142
Version control system......11

virtual..........38, 47, 124, 133
virtual company...............124
virtual server.....................47
virtual server list..............38
Visual SourceSafe.............11
VSS 2005...........................11
warehouse......23, 34, 50, 67,
    80, 112
Warning\...............................
    Application Event Viewer
   31
Web portal problems......184
wildcards..........................115
window handles..............139
WMS - Reduced Picks.(and
    Close)..........................128
work center..........75, 82, 89
workspaceId....................139
workspaces.......................139
write access.....................100
Write method...................131
WSS site.............................46
X++. 8, 40, 42, 118, 125, 129,
    133, 136, 149, 155, 166,
    169, 180
X++ enabled......................42
XGantt ActiveX.................59
Zero $ assets.....................76
zone...................................61
.NET assembly.................155
.NET Business Connector 20
.Net security level.............61
'blank' transactions.........128
'Consumption' field..........50
'edit/create' restriction.....74
'end' flag...........................89
'native' compatibility mode
....53
'Proposal' field..................50
'Quantity' drop list............87
'Release' parameter..........50
'1 per 3 tier' user
    connections................93
'ExecuteSection' method. 151

'go Live'.............................83

www.ingramcontent.com/pod-product-compliance
Lightning Source LLC
Chambersburg PA
CBHW071120050326
40690CB00008B/1282